This timely collection of inquiring essays and interviews focuses critical attention on a major southern writer whose works until quite recently have been in a period of eclipse.

Showing the resurgence of interest in his works, *Erskine Caldwell Reconsidered* examines the present state of Caldwell's reputation and the continuing value of his writings. Here a number of leading Caldwell scholars look at essential details in his career and reappraise Caldwell both as an artist and as a public figure.

With the exception of John Hersey's tribute, the pieces in this collection are original works written expressly for this study. They are examples of the best in Caldwell scholarship of the present time.

Erskine Caldwell Reconsidered gives concentrated attention to Caldwell's personal life. Since no definitive biography has yet been published and since the facts of his life are too little known or shrouded in myth, this collection makes an important contribution to the study of both Caldwell and the time in which he wrote.

Interviews with two of his four wives give additional dimension to the essays and probe Caldwell's biography and his fiction for a better understanding of the man who wrote *Tobacco Road, God's Little Acre*, and other books that generated a wide range of admiration and controversy.

Erskine Caldwell Reconsidered

Erskine Caldwell Reconsidered
Edited by Edwin T. Arnold

University Press of Mississippi
Jackson and London

Southern Quarterly Series

Copyright © 1990 by *The Southern Quarterly*
All rights reserved
Manufactured in the United States of America
93 92 91 90   4 3 2 1
The paper in this book meets the guidelines for permanence and durability of the Committee
on Production Guidelines for Book Longevity of the Council on Library Resources.

Library of Congress Cataloging-in-Publication Data

Erskine Caldwell reconsidered / edited by Edwin T. Arnold.
    p. cm.
   ISBN 0-87805-432-4 (alk. paper) : $17.95
   1. Caldwell, Erskine, 1903- . 2. Authors, American—20th
century—Biography. I. Arnold, Edwin T.
PS3505.A322Z565 1990
813'.52—dc20
 [B]   89-49307
                                                  CIP

British Library Cataloguing-in-Publication data available

Contents

Erskine Caldwell Reconsidered

Oil portrait of Erskine Caldwell by Francis H. Beaugureau, 1955. Courtesy of Virginia Caldwell.

Introduction

When Erskine Caldwell died at the age of 83 on 11 April 1987, the world took note, but in a perfunctory manner. To be sure, there had been a gracious article by Charles Trueheart in *The Washington Post* on March 1 of that year entitled, somberly, "Erskine Caldwell: The Final Chapter," and *USA Today* had sent a reporter and photographer to capture the sick old man in his last days, fighting and losing this third onslaught of cancer. But when he died, there seemed little new to add: Caldwell had been out of the public eye for some time, and the obituaries had all been written long before.

Which is not to say that Caldwell himself had retreated from the world. He had, on the contrary, continued to write and to travel, to give talks and receive awards. He had served as a Montgomery Fellow at Dartmouth College in 1980. In 1981 he was given the Republic of Poland's Order of Cultural Merit; in 1983 the Republic of France named him as a Commander of the Order of Arts and Letters; in 1984 he was elected, with Norman Mailer, to the fifty-chair body of the American Academy of Arts and Letters. In May 1985 he, along with other native writers such as James Dickey, John Oliver Killens and Harry Crews, was honored by the University of Georgia at its *Roots in Georgia* conference. He spent the last years of his life working on his autobiography, *With All My Might*, which was published in France in the fall of 1986 and in this country by Peachtree Press in the month before his death. But this flurry of activity and celebration failed to offset the general neglect of the last few decades of his life. As he said, more to himself than to those standing around him at the University of Georgia conference, "I hate to go in bookstores any more. I hate to see how many of my books aren't there."

It is generally agreed that, although Caldwell wrote and published for almost sixty years, he was primarily a writer of the Depression Era. These were the times that gave him a subject and a cause, that acknowledged him as a spokesman, that most admired the stark power and uniqueness of his art. There was, of course, also the notoriety that arose from his sexual frankness, his willingness to confront the dehumanizing effects of extreme poverty, to represent the absurd and the outrageous and the shocking, without the pretense of moral superiority or affected sentimentality. One finds in such novels as *Tobacco Road*, *God's Little Acre*, *Journeyman*, *Trouble in July*, *Georgia Boy* and *Tragic Ground* and in such stories as "Saturday Afternoon," "Kneel to the Rising Sun,"

4

"Daughter," "The Negro in the Well" and "The Growing Season" a masterful control which, rather than mitigate the inherent outrage, sustains it far beyond any initial sense of shock or disbelief or humor or embarrassment. These are the types of works Faulkner had in mind in 1955 when he ranked Caldwell among those writers he most admired.

But Faulkner also qualified his opinion of Caldwell, as did most of the initial supporters. It was the *early* Caldwell he respected, the *early* Caldwell whose characters, while not totally convincing as people, nevertheless moved him to laughter and to sorrow. Caldwell's later fiction "gradually grew towards trash." It became the commonplace critical line after World War II to denounce Caldwell's work as repetitive, mechanical, shocking for the sake of shock alone. The books sold, but by the late fifties and throughout the sixties, he seemed awfully out of date. He continued to write, and he often wrote very well indeed, but now more often in various forms of nonfiction. At a time in his life and in his career when critical reappraisal would normally have been in order, most scholars in the United States had dismissed him as being unworthy of their concern. He was a minor writer, too long overrated, whose time had passed.

There is, of course, in this overview an element of narrative simplification. Caldwell was never totally forgotten, and there were always the sporadic Caldwell studies that cropped up from time to time, most notably James Korges's monograph *Erskine Caldwell* (University of Minnesota Press, 1969), which, to date, still makes the best case for Caldwell's lasting literary achievement. Within the last decade, other significant publications have appeared, among them the wildly eclectic collection of essays, letters, tributes and memoirs found in the Erskine Caldwell issue of *Pembroke Magazine* (11 [1979]), Scott MacDonald's *Critical Essays on Erskine Caldwell* (G. K. Hall, 1981), James E. Devlin's *Erskine Caldwell* (Twayne, 1984) and my *Conversations with Erskine Caldwell* (University Press of Mississippi, 1988).

Why, then, given Caldwell's present reputation as a writer of secondary importance and the previous existence of substantial scholarship, do we need yet another publication devoted to Caldwell? The most obvious answer is that, with his recent death, we can now begin to see his work as a whole, can begin to develop the perspective that comes with time and closure. Three of the essays in this issue consider Caldwell's career in this fashion. John Hersey's tribute, originally delivered in Caldwell's memory to the American Academy of Arts and Letters, offers the appreciative view of a fellow professional writer. Sylvia Jenkins Cook's essay "Caldwell's Fiction: Growing Towards Trash?" addresses the big question of Caldwell studies: what happened? Her answer analyzes the dangers of success and suggests that Caldwell's growing isolation cut him off from those sources that had engendered his best work. Harvey L. Klevar, in "Caldwell's Women," looks more directly to biography for an answer to this question and argues that Caldwell wrote to satisfy the expectations of the women in his life, from his mother through his four wives.

The kind of biographical emphasis found in Klevar's article offers a second justification for this issue. Although Caldwell led a very long and full life, there has as yet been no published major biography. The personal bits and snatches most often come from Caldwell's own autobiographical writings, but Caldwell was among the most private of men, and writing—or talking—about himself frankly and freely was next to impossible. Neither *Call It Experience* nor *With All My Might* are very satisfying in this sense, and they are, indeed, sometimes misleading. Therefore, a number of these articles stress aspects of Caldwell's personal life in the belief that greater knowledge of the man will lead to a fuller understanding of the artist. In addition to his essay on the women in Caldwell's life, Harvey Klevar, who has long researched Caldwell for a proposed biography, also presents excerpts from interviews he held with the late Helen Caldwell Cushman, Caldwell's first wife. She spoke with great forthrightness about their courtship and marriage and her prominent role in the composition of the early works. Henry Terrie, Professor Emeritus at Dartmouth College, discusses Caldwell's connection with the school and describes the extensive Caldwell Collection held there. Fujisato Kitajima, who refers to himself as "just an ordinary reader and admirer" of Caldwell's works but who, in fact, is an excellent Caldwell translator and bibliographer, explains Caldwell's lasting popularity in Japan and recounts Caldwell's visits there. My interview with Virginia Caldwell concentrates on her husband's last years and the manner in which he faced his death. These articles all reveal information about Erskine Caldwell that has not been commonly available but should be of interest to readers of his books and stories.

Finally, the issue includes two articles which concentrate on specific works. In "Caldwell on Stage and Screen," William L. Howard examines the translation of Caldwell's two most famous novels, *Tobacco Road* and *God's Little Acre*, to other media: Jack Kirkland's stage version and John Ford's film version of *Tobacco Road* and Anthony Mann's film adaptation of *God's Little Acre*. Howard's important thesis is that the stereotypical image often held of Caldwell's plots and characters tends to come from other artists' "revisioning" of Caldwell rather than from what Caldwell actually wrote. Turning to a less well-known book, Ronald Wesley Hoag illustrates in "Canonize Caldwell's *Georgia Boy*: A Case for Resurrection" the kind of thoughtful and perceptive criticism which might be well applied to the many Caldwell books now forgotten and unread. Hoag's essay, though it concentrates on one book, is a general call for reevaluation and thus further supports the underlying motive for this Caldwell issue.

Edwin T. Arnold 7

I would like to express my appreciation to those who have helped me in this project. In addition to the contributors, whose fine work in Caldwell will, I trust, inspire others to join in the scholarship, I would like to thank Virginia Caldwell for her continued cooperation and support. Professor Noel Polk first proposed that I undertake a special Caldwell issue of the *Southern Quarterly*; my thanks to him for that suggestion. My thanks also to Professors Michel Bandry and Scott MacDonald for their advice and encouragement. Philip N. Cronenwett, Curator of Manuscripts/Chief of Special Collections at Dartmouth College Library, in addition to the arduous but gratifying task of cataloging the enormous Caldwell Collection at Dartmouth, graciously took the time to answer my questions and to select from the collection certain of the photographs which appear in this issue. His unique contribution to Caldwell scholarship should never be underestimated or overlooked. I also am indebted to Peggy Prenshaw and Joycelyn Trigg, editor and managing editor of the *Southern Quarterly*, for their suggestions, corrections, enthusiasm and willingness to stretch (but not break) deadlines.

Finally, I would like to express my respect for Professor Masami Nishikawa, eminent scholar, critic and translator of Faulkner, Caldwell and many other American authors. Professor Nishikawa had originally agreed to write on Caldwell's reputation in Japan; his unexpected death in January of 1988 prevented his finishing his essay. Nishikawa and Caldwell were friends for almost thirty years. It was in honor of Professor Nishikawa that Fujisato Kitajima agreed to take up the assignment at a late date, and I am most gratified for the thoroughness of his work.

Edwin T. Arnold

Jeeter could never think of)

The loss of his land and goods ~~could never be thought~~ as anything but a man-made calamity. HE ~~Jeeter~~ sometimes said it was partly his own fault, but he believed steadfastly that his position had been brought about by other people. He did not blame Captain John to the same extent THAT he blamed others, however; Captain John had always treated him fairly, and had done more for him than any other man. When Jeeter had over-bought at the stores in Fuller, Captain John allowed him to CONTINUE ~~~~ and HE never put a limit to the credit allowed. But the end soon came. There was no more profit in raising cotton under the antiquated system HE USED, ~~~~, and he abandoned the farm and moved to Augusta. Rather than attempt to SHOW ~~~~ his tenants HOW TO conform to newer and more economical methods of modern agriculture, which HE THOUGHT would have been AN IMPOSSIBLE ~~~~ task from the start, he sold the stock and implements and moved away. An intelligent employment of his lands, stock, and implements would have enabled Jeeter, and scores Jeeter now was reduced to painful poverty. of others who had become dependent upon him, to raise crops for food and crops to be sold at a profit. Co-operative and corporate farming would have saved them all. His means of livelihood had been taken away, and he was slowly starving.

The entire section of land around him had been originally owned by Jeeter's ~~~~ grandfather. Seventy-five years before, it had been the most desirable soil in the entire west-central part of Georgia. His grandfather had cleared the greater part of the plantation for the production of tobacco. The soil was better suited to the cultivation of tobacco AT THAT TIME than it was for any other crop. It was a sandy loam, and the ridge was high and dry. Hundreds of tumbled-down tobacco barns, chinked with clay, could still be found on what was left of the plantation; some

Sample page of typescript of *Tobacco Road* with Caldwell's handwritten corrections and additions. Photo courtesy of Dartmouth College Library.

Tribute to Erskine Caldwell*

JOHN HERSEY

Erskine Caldwell was born poor on 17 December 1903, in a tiny three-room manse at a mere crossroads in cotton country in Coweta County, Georgia. His father, Ira Sylvester Caldwell, was an Associate Reformed Presbyterian minister, whose salary was $350.00 a year. His mother, Caroline Bell Caldwell, had been a teacher of English and Latin in seminaries and colleges for girls and young women in the Carolinas and Virginia. His grandfathers were a cotton farmer and a railroad telegrapher.

Reverend Caldwell was frequently moved from parish to parish, in Georgia, the Carolinas, Tennessee and Virginia. Erskine's mother taught him at home; he begged to be allowed to go to public schools, but she was convinced that she was better qualified than the teachers Erskine would have drawn in rural schools. Through his childhood, she dressed him in bizarre homemade clothes—a long white linen blouse with a loose leather belt, and bloomer-like trousers. She kept him in curly ringlets until her older sister, a registered nurse, on a visit, gave her a sedative to put her to sleep and took Erskine out to have a haircut. When he was thirteen, he showed his parents a twenty-two page "novel" he had written, and they were so shocked by his spelling that they finally decided to send him to school.

In those young years Erskine saw with his own eyes both the degradation and the inner riches of the very poor, both white and black, in the cotton and tobacco South. His most cherished playmate, for whom he yearned, in a way, all his life, was a black friend named Bisco. After Caldwell was sixty, he wrote a nostalgic book, *In Search of Bisco*. While he was still a boy his father, riding his circuits, took Erskine with him as he made pastoral calls in tenant shacks and hovels. The son would never forget witnessing footwashing services, a clay-eating communion ritual, a coming-through orgy, a snake-handling performance, and emotion-charged glossolalia and unknown-tongue spectacles.

From his youngest years, he fought being poor. As a small boy, he peddled bluing to black washerwomen for ten cents a packet. He scavenged and sold scrap

---

*Tribute to Caldwell at the American Academy of Arts and Letters, 4 December 1987. First published in the *Proceedings of the American Academy and Institute of Arts and Letters*, Second Series, Number 38, Spring, 1988. Copyright 1988.

rubber. He substituted illegally for a village postmaster. At thirteen he took a job as driver of a YMCA auto at an army base in Tennessee. At fifteen, he got a night job shoveling cottonseed in an oil mill in Georgia, alongside young blacks who by day were houseboys or yardmen for whites, and whose tales made the job, as he would later write, "a seminar devoted to the theory and practice of male and female aberrant relationships in an American small town." In later years he would be— intermittently with his writing and obviously enriching it—a stockman in a Kresge store, a cotton picker, a cook, a waiter, a taxi driver, a sodajerk, a stonemason, a professional football player, a bodyguard, a stagehand in a burlesque theatre and a hand on a boat running guns to a Central American country in revolt.

When he was sixteen, while his family was living in Wrens, Georgia, he got a job turning the hand press of the local weekly newspaper, the *Jefferson Reporter*; he was soon allowed to set type by hand, and then to write short news items. And suddenly, with so little to go on, he knew who and what he was. It was no time before he was sending reports of local semi-pro baseball games to the *Augusta Chronicle*, and then sending general news pieces to that paper and to the *Atlanta Constitution*, the *Savannah News* and the *Macon Telegraph*.

Caldwell's higher education consisted of entering and dropping out of two colleges. The first was called Erskine College—named, as he himself was, for the founder of his father's sect, one Ebenezer Erskine—in the town of Due West, South Carolina. Later, having run off to Louisiana and having landed in jail for vagrancy, and having dabbled at various jobs, including journalism, he discovered the existence of a long-forgotten scholarship at the University of Virginia for lineal descendants of soldiers in the Confederate Army. Having somehow established a claim to it, he was admitted in spite of his abysmal academic record. There, in the college library, he helped himself to the only true education he thought he needed, first in little magazines, *transition, This Quarter, The Prairie Schooner*; then in novels, *Sister Carrie, In Our Time, Winesburg, Ohio*.

When he thought he had learned enough to make a start, he married a graduate student named Helen Lannigan, dropped out again, took a job as a reporter for the *Atlanta Journal* and wrote short stories in "spare" time. Three years later, in 1928, he moved with Helen and their two baby sons to a small house in Maine, where he planted vegetables, chopped firewood and wrote short stories. Winter came and they had almost nothing to live on. He had arranged to review books for the *Charlotte Observer* and the *Houston Post*. The person who had set this up for him sent scores and scores of review copies, which he sold to a bookstore in Portland for twenty-five cents each. The family nearly starved; they ate potatoes and rutabagas he had grown the previous summer, and scant groceries bought with the money from reviews and the sale of the books. He wrote in an unheated upstairs room wearing a navy watch cap pulled down over his ears, a sweater, a leather jerkin and a padded storm coat, and with a woolen blanket wrapped around his legs.

He had collected several shoeboxes full of rejection slips when, at last, *transition* accepted ''Midsummer Passion,'' a story which has since had many lives in anthologies. Alas, *transition* paid nothing. But Maxwell Perkins, then editing *Scribner's Magazine*, saw the story and wrote him. He sent Perkins a story a day for a week. Perkins rejected them all, so Caldwell slowed down and sent him two stories a week until, finally, Perkins accepted two. He told Caldwell he would pay ''two-fifty'' for both of them. Caldwell said, ''Two-fifty? I don't know. I thought I'd receive a little more than that.'' Perkins offered three-fifty. ''I guess that'll be all right,'' Caldwell said. ''I'd thought I'd get a little more than three dollars and a half, though, for both of them.'' ''Oh, no!'' Perkins said. ''I must have given you the wrong impression, Caldwell. I meant three hundred and fifty dollars.''

That marked a turning point. Caldwell would never be desperately hard up again. With a boost from Alfred Kreymborg, who with Lewis Mumford and Paul Rosenfeld edited the *New American Caravan*, and who had liked a story of his, he found a publisher for a short novel he had written, entitled *The Bastard*. No sooner was it out than it was attacked as obscene; it was ordered shipped out of Maine within forty-eight hours.

Three years and three books later came *Tobacco Road*, which was even more violently attacked. At first it sold only a few thousand copies, and Caldwell, discouraged, wrote a book with a Maine setting, called *A Lamp for Nightfall*, which wasn't published for twenty years. He had just finished writing *God's Little Acre* when he was invited by MGM to Hollywood, at what seemed to him the astounding salary of $250.00 a week—the first of several stints as a screenwriter that he, like Faulkner, Fitzgerald, West and others, would undertake over the years. Then Jack Kirkland's stage adaptation of *Tobacco Road* opened on Broadway and put Caldwell on easy street. It ran seven and a half years and brought him $2,000.00 every week.

And so he was free to do whatever he wanted, and what he wanted was to roam and to write. The peripatetic life of his childhood had imprinted him with vagabondage. I have counted twenty-eight homes in which he lived, and there were probably others. He had four wives and many secretaries. After his first nine books (published in six years) his restlessness took him on the road to do a picture-and-text book about American types with the photographer Margaret Bourke-White. He left Helen to marry and work with her, but she turned out to be even more a wanderer than he, and they parted. Soon afterward he met an undergraduate at the University of Arizona named June Johnson, and married her, but it turned out that she *hated* to travel; they divorced. On New Year's Eve, 1958, he married his secretary and editorial assistant Virginia Fletcher, and with her he would live, in truth, happily ever after. She was perfectly attuned to his metronomic life: six months each year of writing, six to see the world. She embedded a paradox of serenity in his restlessness.

He roved for the sake of his writing, keeping journals wherever he went. "The need to write fiction," he would report, "had become as demanding as the craving for food when hungry. . . . I had never known a time . . . when I was unable to write a short story or a novel for lack of an idea and suitable material." And indeed it came about that in the years between the publication of his fourth book, *Tobacco Road*, in 1933, and the publication of his fifty-fifth book, *With All My Might*, in 1987, Erskine Caldwell became the most widely read living author on earth. Up to the time of his death this year, eighty million copies of his books had been sold, in forty languages.

How do we account for such an extraordinary outcome? The easy answer, most frequently given: what he wrote was sexy; it was salacious, pornographic. But that won't wash. In terms of explicit sex, *Tobacco Road*, read today in comparison, let's say, with John Updike's *Couples*, is as mild as a Sunday School picnic. It is true that much of Caldwell's writing has a hot erotic power, but it is delicately delivered, and even in the relatively puritanical '30s, among all the charges of obscenity and pornography brought against his early books in New York, Boston, Philadelphia, Cleveland, Detroit, Chicago and elsewhere, only twice were permanent legal bans imposed. The mayor of Chicago succeeded in banning the play of *Tobacco Road*, and Boston's Watch and Ward Society achieved a ban against *God's Little Acre*. "I didn't consider that I was doing something that I shouldn't," Caldwell said in an rare interview four years ago. "I just thought it was natural to make a story as compelling as possible."

Was it because of his compassion for the downtrodden of this world— because he was a proletarian novelist, in the best sense, in times of great suffering and change? It is true that when he went to the Soviet Union with Margaret Bourke-White he was given so many rubles for his Russian royalties that he could afford a luxurious suite at the National Hotel, in the astonishing oval parlor of which there were a grand piano, a bearskin rug and amorous cupids on the ceiling. But Caldwell disavowed this role and was steadfastly apolitical all his life. "I was not trying to prove anything," he was to say. "I was only trying to tell a story."

He chose the right word to account for his success: his best work is indeed compelling. Its surface is very plain, but, reading it, one has a sensation of diving deep into a vivid dream. At the edge of terror, sweet wishes come close to fulfillment, and then drift tantalizingly away. This is very often the case in his short stories, some of which—such as "Kneel to the Rising Sun," "Candyman Beechum," "Country Full of Swedes"—are classics of narrative power. "By an astounding trick of oversimplification," Kenneth Burke wrote, "Caldwell puts people into complex situations while making them act with the scant, crude tropisms of an insect—and the result is cunning.'' Crafty, that is to say, balanced on a razor's edge between hilarity and horror. And all is told in a quiet conversational voice, which speaks in the rhythms of truth.

Caldwell kept himself apart, striving for these effects. ''The fewer writers you know,'' he said once, ''the easier it is to avoid being caught up in that mishmash of literaryism which to me is a very deadly kind of existence.'' Faulkner once named him as one of the five best contemporary writers, along with Hemingway, Dos Passos, Wolfe and himself. An interviewer asked Caldwell if that high ranking pleased him. ''I never think in those terms,'' he said. ''I'm just an ordinary writer, I'm nothing special; so I don't have to have that kind of appreciation. I can do without it. All I'm interested in are the books that I've written. I'm just the writer. The books speak for themselves.''

Erskine Caldwell. Photo taken for the Phoenix Press Club gallery of Life Members, 1951. Courtesy of Virginia Caldwell.

Caldwell's Women

HARVEY L. KLEVAR

Readers and critics familiar with the canon of Erskine Caldwell's writings appreciate the range of his literary modes—fiction, photojournalism, autobiography and experience-based, reflective works. Those, however, who resonated first to the vitality of his early fiction are often disappointed, saddened and puzzled after reading any of Caldwell's post-thirties novels or short stories. Even the most casual readers may find it difficult to believe that the man who wrote *Tobacco Road*, *God's Little Acre* and a bounty of quality short stories in the thirties also authored pieces as slight as *The Sure Hand of God* in the forties, *Gretta* in the fifties or *Annette* in the seventies. Certainly none of the fiction Caldwell struggled to write during the last four decades of his life approached the promise which his early work had encouraged literary critics and loyal Caldwell readers to anticipate.

Only six years after the issue of *Tobacco Road* (1932), Caldwell's first major novel, critics such as Louis Untermeyer, Lewis Gannet and Joseph Wood Krutch commonly celebrated his talent. They predicted that Caldwell, along with Faulkner, Hemingway and O'Hara, would take up the American literary torch from the likes of Thoreau, James and Howells. In sum, they collegially estimated that Caldwell's fictional talents were the most original and substantial among contemporary American writers. Many years and books later, however, Malcolm Cowley, always a sympathetic Caldwell critic, accurately measured the harvest of those expectations: "It is the early books—say the first three novels and stories up to *Georgia Boy* (1943)—on which his [literary] reputation will stand or fall" (131).

If Caldwell's promise in the late thirties seemed so great, why did it fail to flower as anticipated? Those others with whom Caldwell's talent was often compared—Faulkner and Hemingway, Steinbeck or even O'Hara—managed through their lifetimes at least to maintain, if not to enhance, their respective literary credentials. Caldwell's post-thirties fiction, sadly enough, proved his inability to do likewise. But with the exception of a single work—*Love and Money* (1954)—the clues to the causes of his failure are not to be discovered in his writings themselves. Rather they are to be found in his life story. There we discover that the catalyst which first fueled Caldwell's creative surge and later compromised it was his essential dependence upon women. More than anything else, he yearned for their love and approval. Always fearful that he could not be loved for himself, he tried to earn love by becoming whatever he intuited that women wanted him to

15

be. And so it was that Caldwell strove to merit the love of that succession of women in his life: first his mother, and later each of his four wives.

Caldwell was the only child of a humane Associated Reformed Presbyterian minister and his conscientiously dutiful wife. From the time he was born on 17 December 1903 until his fourteenth year, Caldwell moved with his parents from place to place in the South. As a trouble-shooting arbiter for his denomination, Ira Sylvester (or I. S., as his son always called him), was shifted by his presbytery from one troubled rural church to another. Seldom did the family stay in one location for more than a few months at a time. Always the staunchly proper wife and mother, Caroline Preston Bell Caldwell accompanied her husband to those assignments where in her words she "suffered, bled, and worse than died backing him" (Undated notes).

Because of Rev. Caldwell's position, the Caldwells were usually considered outsiders by the troubled congregations and communities. As an official mediator between warring church factions, I. S. had to avoid friendships or associations that might have been perceived as affecting his impartiality. Erskine and his mother, who was unable to have other children, were thus thrust into a situation of almost exclusive interdependence. Without a role in the church, without a circle of close friends and almost always alone with the child, Caroline assumed the role of the constantly caring mother. A moment of carelessness subsequently made her an even more vigilant and protective parent. While Erskine was still eating from a high chair, he pulled a pot of hot cooking grease onto himself from the stove. After months of Caroline's around-the-clock ministering, the doctor told her, "Considering the close calls this child has had, the good Lord must be saving him for something special" (V. Caldwell letter).

Thereafter, Carrie treated her son as someone destined for greatness. She, along with her female relatives who sometimes cared for Erskine, granted him masculine exemptions and privileges he came to expect as his due. Those were countered, nonetheless, by rigid considerations which made her son seem not so much special as different. He was seldom allowed to go barefoot. She refused to have his hair cut so that he wore long curly, red locks until age eight when I. S. spirited him to a barber without his wife's knowledge. More crucially, because she did not want her son influenced by the rustic language and behavior common in local rural schools, she taught him at home herself. He consequently did not interact with other children in a school setting until his mother finally enrolled him, at the age of twelve, in a private academy in Salem, Tennessee.

Despite her love for Erskine, Caroline was a demanding mother who could not express warmth and affection. He therefore learned that duty was a form of righteousness, that reason more than emotion should regulate a person's life. The

Caldwell with his Aunt Sallie Bell and a neighbor child in Staunton, Virginia (no date). Photo courtesy of Dartmouth College Library.

child also discovered that if he disappointed her, he would be subjected to long punishing silences. Such exactions encouraged what was to become a lifelong habit of solitude. On at least two occasions he ran away from home, and both times it was his father who found him and carried him back.

When Caldwell was fourteen, the family settled in Wrens, Georgia, where Caroline shortly began teaching English and I. S. both ministered and taught part-time. There he is remembered as a quiet youth, often alone. Leaving high school at age sixteen, a few credits short of graduation, Caldwell enrolled at Erskine College, his father's alma mater. His record there confirms what he subsequently claimed—that he spent more time away from campus gathering experiences than he did attending classes. After a few years of being in and out of that institution, Caldwell enrolled at the University of Virginia where he did not improve upon his record. By this time he was twenty-one and still confused and directionless.

Caldwell convinced his parents that taking summer classes at the Wharton School of Economics in Philadelphia would allow him better to understand those economic forces which dictated American experience. They paid his train fare and he thereafter supported himself with part-time jobs. When the summer ended, Caldwell enrolled in more courses at Lehigh University. Though he passed all four classes taken at both institutions, his record argued a continued confusion and lack of direction. Just as certainly, it reflected no interest in either literature or creative writing of any sort.

Yet Caldwell's almost six months' experience in Philadelphia and Wilkes-Barre is remarkable as a preface for what was to follow. Though letters to his parents justified the wisdom of his Philadelphia sojourn, they also bemoaned his hardships and hinted of a loneliness which later provided *The Sacrilege of Alan Kent* (1936) with its motive force. He yearned for women he saw but could not have. Caldwell has Alan Kent admit, ''I had no place to go and nothing now to do. Almost everybody else I saw had someone who loved him and they were happy together'' (*Sacrilege* 54). What more Caldwell felt can only be inferred from a cryptic admission he made in a letter to his parents: ''I've found out what it means not to have a home you can go to at night'' (6 June 1924). He then begged his parents' aid in returning to the University of Virginia for the term beginning in January 1925.

Caldwell's registration materials at the university listed ''business'' as his intended occupation, and he signed up for four courses extending over two terms. At the end of those combined periods he had salvaged only two barely passing grades from among the eight possible. More than indirection confounded Caldwell during that time. Early that January he had met Helen Lannigan, the attractive eighteen-year-old daughter of the University of Virginia track coach. Precocious and bright, Helen already had earned an undergraduate degree in English from William and Mary and was a second-year graduate student in French at Virginia when the two met.

Caldwell intrigued Helen. Tall and husky, red-haired and laconic, he projected a smoldering intensity which appealed to her. Within a few weeks they were sleeping together. Helen additionally was moved by ''his burning desire'' to be a writer (Interview). A few weeks before he had intended to go into business. Why then had he presented himself to her as a writer-to-be?

Caldwell seems to have intuited that the notion of the aspiring writer would appeal to Helen. Certainly Caldwell had toyed with the idea of writing in the past. During one of his Erskine College leaves, he had been the Wrens string correspondent for a Savannah paper. Moreover, his respectable mother had written and published poetry and appreciated literature. His father also wrote for newspapers and sociological publications. So for Helen's sake, to gain her love, Caldwell apparently took on the author's role. It was important that he play the part well, for he wanted more than a casual sexual relationship with her. Later, she guessed that he had been ''seeking a home, a sense of security'' (Interview), as indeed his Wilkes-Barre confession had admitted.

Under pressure from Caldwell, who wanted ''to make an honest woman of her,'' Helen agreed to elope with him little more than two months after they had met (Interview). They married on 20 March 1925, during the midst of presidential inauguration festivities in Washington, D.C. The young couple lived with the Lannigans until the semester's end. Then Caldwell's father, using his contacts, got his son a reporter's job with the *Atlanta Journal*, but the couple was barely settled before Helen discovered that she was pregnant. As a cub reporter he earned little and quickly recognized that his situation provided less than he had promised Helen and wanted for himself. The examples of two other *Journal* reporters, however, offered an alternative. Margaret Mitchell and Francis Newman both had novels in process. Through the intercession of a friend, Caldwell began reading the pages for *The Hard Boiled Virgin* as Newman completed them. That experience, combined with the poor quality of the many books he and Helen reviewed to supplement their income, convinced them that Caldwell could do as well.

Abandoning the security of an assured twenty-five dollars per week, the Caldwells, including their new son, Erskine Preston, moved to the Lannigan's summer home in Mount Vernon, Maine. There they determined that Erskine would write without other work distractions. Helen encouraged that gamble despite the hardships it thrust upon her because she recognized his ''overwhelming obsession to write. . . . It was the one thing he hoped to do in life'' (Interview).

After the first Maine summer produced nothing publishable, the Caldwells returned to Virginia and the Lannigan household. There he enrolled in another year of courses at the University. And there he claimed to have come alive in Atcheson Hench's writing seminar, comparing himself to "a haystack on the verge of bursting into flames" (Letter to Hench). That inspiration notwithstanding, Caldwell's struggles to write continued. Shunting his growing family seasonally between Maine and Georgia, he wrote for three years without any published rewards. By the spring of 1929 he admitted in a letter to his father, "If I could only get a piece accepted by an important magazine or publisher, it would be easier to have hopes. . . . I have been trying to write for a long time and it is becoming discouraging" (19 Mar. 1929).

That Helen so enthusiastically supported and respected Caldwell's now very real writing aspirations is crucial to an understanding of his career. She endured more than eight years of grinding poverty for the sake of his art. As their family grew to three children, she almost exclusively cared for them so their demands and exuberances would not disturb him. To give him greater peace, she supported his move to a small guest house near the lake and away from the big house. There she would bring him his meals and occasionally spend the night. Later, when Caldwell proved unfaithful to her, Helen would forgive him. Throughout their marriage she granted Caldwell large exceptions because, like his mother before, she believed him to be "special" and treated him accordingly. His "genius . . . removed him from the human equation," she believed; he could not be judged "by the same standards you'd judge an ordinary human being" (Interview).

Caldwell thus enjoyed a latitude of privilege and forgiveness accorded to few people. Conversely, however, this privilege carried with it covert expectations and demands. Had Caldwell not succeeded as a writer, he might have lost his privileges along with the respect and love which fed them. Or so it could have seemed to one who had always been loved because he was considered "special."

Helen provided more than companionship, a compatible home environment and encouragement during Caldwell's early writing years. Intelligent, astute and direct, she was, at first, his lone reader. In fact she "was a natural for Erskine" because she not only "corrected everything he wrote" but also "even used to type his damn stuff" (Interview). Her language skills, her familiarity with southern folk and their dialects and her acquaintance with Maine's "Down Easters" all allowed her to determine whether or not a story rang true. Although the stories Caldwell wrote were his and his alone, all imaginatively refined from his wealth of experiences, justice demands that Helen's contributions not be overlooked. Only the fiction Caldwell wrote while married to her received more than lukewarm critical acclaim.

By the end of 1929, Caldwell's fortunes had turned. Small journals accepted three of his short stories for publication, and Heron Press had agreed to publish his apprentice novel, *The Bastard*. By the next spring Maxwell Perkins had accepted two stories for *Scribner's Monthly* for payment of $350.00. Caldwell wrote to share his elation with his parents: "I've got this far, and I've got to go further. . . . I am working for the Pulitzer Prize, so help me God!" (24 Mar. 1930).

Caldwell was never to win that or any other major critical award for his writing. Yet the Scribner's boost marked the beginning of the most fruitful literary years he was to enjoy. Between 1930 and 1936 all of those works that established Caldwell's critical reputation were released. Scribner's published his short-story collection *American Earth* (1931) and his first major novel, *Tobacco Road* (1932). Subsequently Viking Press issued *God's Little Acre* (1933), *Journeyman* (1935) and two short-story collections: *We Are the Living* (1933) and *Kneel to the Rising Sun* (1935). *The Sacrilege of Alan Kent* (1936) defied fictional categorization. As a work tracing Caldwell's beginnings, however, it served as a fitting conclusion to the most productive literary period of his life. In fact, after 1936 four years were to pass before he was to write more than occasional pieces of fiction. By then Caldwell's personal situation had so essentially changed that thereafter he could never retrace those patterns which had shaped his early fiction.

Caldwell's first and chief success came from his representation of the poor and dispossessed. Not since the works of George Washington Harris and Mark Twain had any American author written with such sympathy and humor about these people. What made Caldwell's treatment unique was the empathy with which he so obviously traced the comedy, tragedy and idiosyncrasies of his fictional characters. As marginal survivors, their lives, through Caldwell's fiction, resonated with cosmic, social and psychological forces which gave universal meaning to otherwise impoverished existences. When Caldwell wrote out of his experience, first in Georgia and later in Maine, his fiction was affective and arresting. His keen eye and ear caught the nuances of behavior and speech that characterized the poor whites and blacks of the South as well as the back-country inhabitants of rural Maine. His sparse prose created a stark reality that lodged in the reader's mind.

But the coming of literary success and critical acclaim promoted changes in Caldwell's life. Although he and Helen continued to live in near destitution until the spring of 1933, their circumstances thereafter altered dramatically. First one Hollywood writing assignment, then later another, and finally the royalties from the very successful stage version of *Tobacco Road* meant that Caldwell would never have to live in poverty again. Certainly that luxury distanced him from the poor whose grim realities previously had not been so totally alien to his own.

Ultimately, however, it was not just a distancing from the poor that diminished the quality of Caldwell's fiction. Rather, it was a distancing from Helen which was to confound it. The degree to which he relied upon her first became obvious during his three-month film assignment in Hollywood in 1933. He wrote her to do all she could with the *Journeyman* typescript so it would "be finished as far as [she was] concerned" (7 May 1933). Later, as Viking Press urged the hurried completion of the *We Are the Living* collection, Caldwell worried. He needed her help in choosing the stories to be included (17 June 1933). She was to reread *Journeyman* to see if she "could find something wrong with it" (12 July 1933). And finally, he wished she "could have read it at least once" before it went to the press (29 July 1933). She, no doubt, could have found much to improve the book.

    And so Helen most likely would have continued to contribute to Caldwell's career had their marriage endured. But that was not to be, a fact that made all the difference as far as his literary future was concerned.

    By 1936 reviewers and critics of Caldwell's writings commonly accused him of creating grotesques, of promoting sensationalism and exaggeration in his fiction. Caldwell wished to prove them wrong. A photojournal book focused upon the southern prototypes of people like those who stalked his landscapes would, he felt, vindicate him. The person chosen to work with Caldwell in this venture was Margaret Bourke-White, a vivaciously attractive photographer for *Life* magazine. Less than two weeks into their late spring travels through the deep South, Caldwell and Bourke-White had entered into a relationship whose depth was to surprise them both. After their three weeks together, Helen intuited what had happened and realized that this was no casual affair like the others in which Caldwell had dallied.

    Caldwell himself was torn between love and duty on one hand and love and passion on the other. When with Helen, he wrote plaintive love letters to Margaret. With Margaret, he wrote yearning letters to Helen begging her patience and understanding. She was to "keep a stiff-upper lip . . . until something happened" (22 Apr. 1937). His situation was "something like being given a term on the chain gang, maybe" (10 May 1937). He loved her and missed what they should be having together, but he could not help himself.

    Finally Helen granted Caldwell a year of grace to see if he could get Margaret out of his system. She allowed him to continue living first with Margaret and then with her. During the first two months of 1937, Caldwell wrote four stories and mailed them to Helen with instructions: "If you are satisfied with them, correct them and send them to [Maxim] Lieber [his literary agent] right away" (1 Mar. 1937). These were the last pieces of fiction Caldwell was to write for three years.

    A new love demanded that he reshape his interests and career to satisfy Bourke-White's expectations and professional obligations. Though she loved Caldwell with as much passion as he loved her, she refused to compromise her art. If he wished, he could accompany her on her photography assignments, but she would not limit her career for him or any other love.

For a year Caldwell vacillated between Helen and Margaret. When Bourke-White was on assignment, he lived with Helen and the children in Maine. From there he wrote letters to Bourke-White: "I can't be satisfied with a part of you. I need all of you all the time to be completely happy. And I want it to be as long as we live" (Feb. 1937). But instead of spending a lifetime with Margaret, he could be with her only during those periods when she was in New York, not nearly enough to satisfy his needs.

Like his mother before, Caldwell used long silences to punish those who claimed to love him but who would not bend to his "special" needs. Such tactics had worked with Helen, but they did not move Margaret. Instead she demanded that he see a psychiatrist if he wanted their relationship to continue. So he did—once. Then, rather than submit to more psychic probing, Caldwell decided to begin traveling with Margaret. In the early spring of 1937, the two of them went back to the Deep South for more documentary evidence to support what was to be their photojournalistic study of poverty, *You Have Seen Their Faces*. Upon their return to New York they labored over the photo selection and manuscript. According to Helen's testimony, they requested that she come to their New York place to help edit the book (Interview).

Shortly thereafter, Caldwell and Margaret departed for a three-month assignment in California. For weeks Caldwell's parents had heard nothing from their son. Worried, they ferreted the truth from Helen about Caldwell's relationship with Margaret and their location. Caroline's letter to Helen cast the blame even as it tallied the costs: "I feel that he had been trapped and double crossed. No wonder he could not write anything worthwhile" (3 Sept. 1937). But to her son she wrote, "Living up there in Maine the year round has put you in an intolerable position. You need to have daily contact with MEN—not women of whom I have poor opinion." After the excuse came the forgiveness: "If you need any help that we have in our power to give, let us know" (9 Aug. 1937).

That forgiveness was a grace Caldwell expected from all who loved him. Yet Margaret was not so pliable. Returning from California, the two had an argument in New Mexico. Angered, she left him there with his car. He subsequently became so ill he called Helen for help. She and the youngest child, Janet, went by train down to his rescue, and Helen drove him back to New York, to be with Margaret. Though Caldwell perhaps avoided tallying the larger costs of his obsession with Margaret, Helen did not. "You can never know how much I miss you and all we had together," she wrote. "I miss so much our trips, our long talks about your work, our working over and over on your stories" (23 Jan. 1938). Shortly thereafter, nonetheless, Helen filed for a divorce. When it was granted on 18 April 1938, Caldwell was with Margaret in Czechoslovakia. He had accompanied her there to compile a photo essay study of Eastern Europe on the brink of war.

For a long while Caldwell had not written any "worthwhile" fiction. He had been too unsettled to write more than the texts for *You Have Seen Their Faces* (1937) and *North of the Danube* (1939). Though both works earned glowing reviews (but limited sales), they were not fiction. Neither did they satisfy the editors at Viking Press who had not been able to issue a fresh Caldwell fictional work since 1935. This pressure only added to Caldwell's discontent. Ever since Helen's divorce, he and Margaret had lived together, but she had refused his pleas for marriage. He could not write without that assurance of her love. Finally she relented, but not before having Caldwell sign a prenuptial agreement. Two of its conditions were especially telling. He was "to attempt to realize and control his fluctuating moods" (Bourke-White 171), and he was not to try to seduce her away from her photographic assignments. Caldwell agreed, and they were married on 28 February 1939, almost a year after his divorce from Helen.

Two months later, often alone while Margaret traveled, Caldwell sat in their Darien, Connecticut, house, attempting to rekindle that fictional blaze which had burned so promisingly before he had become involved with her. Unlike his previous novels, the book that was to be *Trouble in July* did not come boiling forth. His letters to "Kit" during her travels bemoaned his need for her. Recognizing his loneliness, his father urged that Caldwell spend time with them while his wife was away. I. S. felt that it was time Caldwell wrote "a great Southern story," but he likewise issued a warning: "At the same time you are not well enough acquainted with the South. You will invariably make mistakes until you get better acquainted" (Letter).

Caldwell ignored his father's advice, even though by this time Margaret had departed for a six-month European assignment. His letters of complaint to her continued: he could not sleep at night; he was "hanging on day after day." If only she would allow him to "take charge" of her, that "would be a very good thing for them" because he knew "a little about how to live" (2 Dec. 1939). Such offers Kit left unanswered. As Caldwell struggled to complete *Trouble*, he even approached her as he once had Helen. He considered her his "best friend and severest critic," and he anticipated her sending some "notes of changes" that would help make the work a better novel (4 Dec. 1939).

But Margaret was no Helen. There is no evidence that, either then or later, she ever helped him critique his fiction. When *Trouble in July* finally appeared, in February of 1940, Margaret still had not returned to help him weather its reviews. Except for Richard Wright and other black critics who praised the book's condemnation of southern racism and violence, most reviewers were not complimentary. They used the book as evidence of Caldwell's "falling off" and berated him for reusing characters and themes from his earlier fiction. An English critic, John Mair, summarized what almost all of Caldwell's future fiction would

Caldwell and Margaret Bourke-White in Moscow, 1941. Photo courtesy of Dartmouth College Library.

confirm: *Trouble in July* marked "the end of a stage in Mr. Caldwell's development." What the reviewer could not know was that the end of that stage had its
beginnings when Caldwell had allied himself to Margaret Bourke-White. Through
that alliance he ultimately divorced himself from both Helen and the South. Each
had been integral to his best fiction.

Margaret's six-month absence confirmed that Caldwell could barely tolerate
life without her or some other love to meet his needs. He had short-term liaisons
with a local married woman and with a Florida coed whom he enticed to
Connecticut. After Margaret finally returned from Europe in April of 1940,
Caldwell would not allow himself to be separated from her for long periods.
During the summer and fall of that year they spent much time together as they
toured the states to collect material for another collaborative volume eventually
issued as *Say, Is This the U.S.A.?* (1941). That long-term association, however,
precipitated some of those same problems that had always haunted their relationship. By late August, Margaret directed her secretary to forward the address of the
psychiatrist whom Caldwell had seen previously.

That same month, Duell, Sloan and Pearce, the firm Caldwell had joined after
leaving Viking Press, issued *Jackpot*, his collection of stories which received
almost universal praise from reviewers and critics and unsolicited congratulatory
letters from Hemingway and Dreiser. No one seemed to notice that only each
story's pithy introduction plus four new pieces represented recently written
fiction.[1]

The *U.S.A.* travels and manuscript completed by February, the Caldwells
rushed to meet a mid-March departure date. Margaret had announced that she
wanted to do a fourth book with him, this time a study of Russia. Caldwell realized
that if he failed to accompany her, he would have to accept another lengthy
separation. They flew from the West Coast to Honolulu, Hong Kong and
Chungking. After being forced down in Mongolia by a Gobi sandstorm, the
Caldwells did not reach Moscow until May of 1941, some six weeks after they had
departed.

Less than two months later, they found themselves to be among a handful of
Americans in Russia when the Germans attacked. There they remained, dodging
Luftwaffe bombs, photographing and writing for *Life* and *PM* newspaper and
making radio broadcasts for CBS about the war. Departing Russia in early October
they arrived in London where they hurried their last collaboration, *Russia at War*
(1942), to a publisher. Four days later, Caldwell had his wartime diary *Moscow
Under Fire* (1942) in manuscript form. Back in Darien by early November,
Caldwell managed to publish eleven short stories he somehow had contrived to
write during his and Margaret's war-punctuated odyssey. A month later he mailed
the manuscript for *All-Out on the Road to Smolensk* (1942), a collection of his

newspaper reports, to Duell, Sloan and Pearce.

By February of 1942, both Caldwell and Bourke-White realized that America's entry into the War would mean more lengthy and far-flung assignments for Margaret. As mid-March and Margaret's European departure date loomed, Caldwell tried to entice her to stay by purchasing a home near Tucson, Arizona. That tactic failed, and he resigned himself to another long separation. With Margaret gone, Caldwell worked to complete *All Night Long* (1942), a novel on Russian guerrilla warfare. Deprived of Margaret's presence, he again invited the Florida coed to return as his companion-aide.

By 1 July 1942, Caldwell had completed the book, closed the house in Darien and driven west with the young woman. Stopping in Hollywood before continuing to Tucson, he discovered his agent Al Manuel had snared a $1,250.00 per week writing contract for him. For some six weeks he worked on the script for *Mission to Moscow*, collected $50,000.00 for the screen rights to *All Night Long* and anticipated settling in at the new Arizona house he had built for Margaret. Because he felt the Florida girl was not valuable to him anymore, he convinced her that her future lay in Hollywood and departed alone.

Caldwell deliberately had planned to isolate himself in Tucson. Ever since meeting Margaret Bourke-White, their pace had proved too frenetic for him to cultivate his fiction writing as congenially as he had in Maine with Helen. He needed undisturbed time and solitude to write himself home again through a humor-laced novel he was to call *Georgia Boy* (1943). But without Helen's companionship and without Margaret's love, Caldwell felt bereft. After just a week alone he advised his parents that if Margaret did not return by the following July, he planned ''to join the army'' (2 Oct. 1942). Four days later, speaking to a writing class at the University of Arizona, he met a pretty and bright young student named June Johnson.

Three weeks later, on 27 October 1942, Caldwell proposed to the twenty-one-year-old college senior in an unusual manner. He sent her a bogus memorandum listing all his financial assets for a net worth in excess of $100,000.00. This he offered as surety that he wished to bestow ''all his love and worldly goods'' upon her (Statement). His appeal was revealing. For Helen's sake he had become a writer, for Margaret's, a wayfaring collaborator. But to secure June's love, he offered his present and future wealth.

In November Caldwell advised his lawyer to file the necessary divorce papers. He could be reached in Mexico City where he would spend the necessary twenty-day Mexican-divorce waiting period finishing *Georgia Boy*, the novel he had begun only during the last week in September. (Five portions of the book had been published previously as separate stories in various magazines.) By 16 December he had finished the book, as he had come there to do. On 20 December he had the divorce decree in hand, and the next day, 21 December 1942, four days after his thirty-ninth birthday, he married June Johnson.

Caldwell's last work while married to Bourke-White, *All Night Long*, had generated no praise even during that war-torn time. Most reviewers agreed with the *Nation* critic who estimated it to be one of the worst novels she had ever read (Marshall). The reviews of *Georgia Boy*, in comparison, hinted that Caldwell's fiction-writing career might yet be resurrected. Though the work paled next to *Tobacco Road*, reviewers felt it was better than anything Caldwell had recently written. Caldwell's fleeting literary resurgence seemed to follow from his altered marital circumstances. At that stage June was no direct-speaking Helen or career-determined Margaret. Rather she was yet a young woman awed by Caldwell's reputation and willing to shape herself to meet his expectations. *Georgia Boy* flowed so easily because marrying June had made him "feel right for the first time" in his life (Letter to Morang, 8 Jan. 1943).

Caldwell continued trying to recapture his talent in his next novel, *Tragic Ground* (1944). In letters to his old friend Alfred Morang, he invariably agonized about his writing and what he might accomplish through it. But the priorities and direction of his life had changed by 1944. The realities of marriage and a new baby boy reshaped June's early accommodations. Moreover, Caldwell's life patterns had also begun to change dramatically. Living as poorly as he and Helen had, money had always been a nagging concern for him, but always his writing had come first. And though money and expenses occupied him during his Bourke-White years, he was so obsessed with Margaret that all else remained secondary.

But during Caldwell's marriage to June, he devoted increasingly more attention and energy toward accumulating wealth. Shortly after the war he joined her father in purchasing an electrical contracting company. On his own he acquired two undeveloped real estate properties. He became the majority shareholder and functioning board chairman of a local radio station which, in time, also expanded into television. And although, like his father before, Caldwell had always driven Fords, he now cruised around in Cadillacs while June sported her Corvette. Because elite social clubs were important to her, he enrolled them in the Tucson Country Club and the Press Club, where he even wrote skits for their amateur shows. He became a charter member of the Saddle and Sirloin Club. Caldwell had adapted to meet June's needs.

As distracting and time-consuming as these activities and associations were, others, far more damaging to his creativity and literary reputation, also compromised his artistic integrity. After the war, Al Manuel, his Hollywood agent and friend, increasingly swayed Caldwell to his own "money-as-measure" norms. He urged him to accept lucrative screenwriting assignments and to participate in

Erskine and June Caldwell, his third wife, Tucson, Arizona, 1944. Photo courtesy of Dartmouth College Library.

flamboyant promotions of the films made from his novels. In addition, Caldwell joined forces with the Penguin-Mentor paperback business. Using the Fawcett Publications comic book distribution system, Penguin-Mentor hawked Caldwell's seductively-covered paperbound books in drugstores and depots across the United States. Signed to a $50,000.00 bonus plus a one-cent per copy royalty, Caldwell shortly was touring the country, standing by drugstore racks "merchandising" and signing the twenty-five cent copies of his works.

Such activities exacted from Caldwell a literary price beyond reckoning. The time and energy lost to his writing was a part of it. A suspect literary notoriety added to it. Newspaper articles and tasteless ads placed by Roscoe Fawcett preceded "the author of *God's Little Acre*" wherever he was sent to vend his books. Arriving at a 1948 University of Kansas writer's conference directly from signing paperbacks in Katz's Kansas City drugstore, Caldwell found himself a pariah among participants such as Katherine Anne Porter, Allan Tate and Caroline Gordon. Later he was defensively boastful as he acknowledged that similar promotional tactics had made him "an outcast among the literary guys" (Letter to Yordan).

And yet tasteless trading upon Caldwell's earlier reputation for money's sake was not the sole cause of his strained literary credibility. Before his seduction by celluloid and paperback moguls, before his marriage to June and all of the "woman anxieties" it eventually provoked, Caldwell had never written a novel with a woman as its central character. After 1945, however, all of his subsequently published eighteen volumes of fiction—save four[2]—featured women protagonists. Though some of those works utilized southern settings and characters, in most instances they were so predictably formulaic that they seemed almost mechanically written. Why Caldwell suddenly switched to writing almost exclusively about lonely women lost in a meaningless world is a puzzle, but not one without telltale clues.

A partial explanation is that Caldwell too uncritically accepted the judgments and direction of his movie and paperback associates. Like today's Harlequin romance writers, he was encouraged to write toward a profitably defined market. Yet despite his regard for money, would Caldwell, who felt he had been "born with the gift" (*Experience* 230), who believed it was a "sacrilege" not to use one's talents, have so consciously prostituted that gift? Some force more personally compelling than money moved Caldwell to write so exclusively about women.

By 1945 his marriage to June was already deeply troubled, a matter he could not understand. Despite his bending every effort to make money for her, despite a nurse for their child and domestic help for the house, she remained unhappy. Her many phone calls and social activities annoyed him. She, on the other hand, could not cope with those brooding silences he exacted as punishments. Seeking her own identity, June attempted, without much success, to build upon her college writing interests. Ultimately Caldwell could not understand why she was not satisfied with being an accommodating accessory to him and his career. He was helplessly confounded by her and by women in general.

Subsequently the Caldwells' marriage continued to deteriorate. More and more Caldwell felt unappreciated and rejected. Since June refused to accompany him, he traveled alone. At the 1948 Kansas Writer's Conference, and thereafter in other places, a young woman reporter for the *Beaumont Enterprise* gave him some of those comforts June denied. By this time Caldwell had completed his third book about women. It was as if he thought that the act of writing would contribute to his understanding of them. June soon began to see a psychoanalyst once a week. Caldwell finally refused to pay the full amount of June's four-hundred-dollar monthly bill. He came to believe that the man had gone beyond his professional boundaries with her. On her part, June pretty much gave Caldwell carte-blanche to do what he wished as long as it did not involve her.

In 1952 Caldwell received a note from a Virginia Moffett Fletcher. While traveling with June three years earlier, he had met Virginia at a publisher's gathering in Maryland. Though she had been attracted to him then, Virginia had left the party without offering him either encouragement or a mailing address. Since that time she and her young son had relocated to Sarasota where she was painting and attempting to rearrange her life after a three-year separation from her husband.   After exchanging correspondence, Caldwell arranged to meet her in Florida in early March. There they talked far into their two nights together. He mused much about June, his feelings of rejection. He compared himself to a turtle; he had been hurt so often he feared coming out of his shell. Reading *The Sacrilege of Alan Kent* as they sat by the pool, Virginia wept. She realized that he had been lonely all his life.

Six weeks after they parted, Caldwell returned to ask if Virginia would consider becoming the fourth Mrs. Erskine Caldwell. Because her seven-year-old came first, she was not sure she would marry again. She already recognized, moreover, that Caldwell's needs would totally consume her life. She agreed, nonetheless, to meet him in June at the Mayo Clinic where he, fearing cancer, was to undergo a battery of tests. Before she arrived, Caldwell, as he had done during the Helen-Margaret quandary, wrote to June: "I want . . . to tell you that I love you and want your love more than anything else in the world. . . . I am lonely without you all the time and I don't understand why life has to be uncomplete [sic] not to be one with you" (Letter).

The next day Virginia arrived for a three-day visit, and happily the tests revealed no cancer. When she left, however, she still had not given any assurances about either marrying him or relocating to Arizona. The following 1 November Caldwell began writing *Love and Money*, a book which, even his editor was to caution, readers might think autobiographical. Written from the first-person point of view, like his *The Sacrilege of Alan Kent*, *Love and Money*, through its protagonist Rick Sutter, probes those anxieties, uncertainties and values which haunted Caldwell during this period of his life and career. Three obsessions preoccupy Sutter: real and ideal "woman," his disappointing writing career and his need for critical self-examination.

Sutter is a writer between books, unable to find a subject for a "different kind of novel" (13) and months behind his self-imposed schedule. In the words of his friend Rob Mizemore, Sutter seeks a woman to sustain him, "mentally, morally, spiritually and physically." This woman must fill "a need—a void" (40) in his life. In Sarasota he finds her, a woman who, like Virginia, has "thick dark hair, cut somewhat short and framing her face" (21) and has a seven-year-old child. Despite an idyllic night the two spend on the sands of Siesta Key, she refuses Sutter's offer of marriage and runs away—to New Orleans, Houston and Colorado Springs, all places where Caldwell himself had had various woman-associations in the past. Sutter follows her in what becomes a quest for not only the ideal woman but also a peaceful resolution of the other anxieties which haunt him.

During the course of that journey Sutter engages in numerous discussions with friends concerning his confusion. Mizemore, a professor-critic, and he celebrate the idea of "woman," with her "mothering instinct" and her "ability and capacity and imagination to be fulfilling of any demand [men] make on her." The hymn of praise concludes with a vision of a perfect woman-mother placed on a pedestal: "There should be a worshipful statue of her at every crossroad, every hamlet, in every public place," his friend says, for "there is nothing to take her place . . . in the life of a normal man" (40). But as another friend tells him, "There's no future in your frantic attempts, when you're between books, to find the ideal woman. There is no such creature . . . you'll never be able to find her because she doesn't exist outside your imagination. Most writers have the same telltale occupational malady—you, too. You get in the habit of making fictional women so attractive and desirable—when you're not making them despicable and crude—that you'll always be disappointed with every last one of them in real life" (145).

Through the professor-critic who serves as a foil to confront both Sutter and Caldwell himself, the writer(s) face a disturbing question: "Is it better to write a poor novel than not write a novel at all?" (41). What if the millions of readers of "some shoddy books" with "not the slightest suggestion of a philosophy of human existence [in them]" are merely "in search of a thrill" (43, 42). The speaker then forces a dark recognition: he tells Sutter that he is "second rate" and advises: "If you can't write better novels in the future than you have in the past, you ought to shut up shop here and now" (43). The critic continues to confront Sutter. He is vain and conceited, selfish, despicable and obnoxious. His personal life reflects the mishmash in his novels, and he is so unstable he cannot stay married. He is but "an inferior human being who is taking up useful space on God's green earth" (43). Toward the novel's conclusion, Caldwell allows Sutter to speak for himself: "Sometimes I think writers like me ought to be kept in cages so they can't mingle with decent human beings. I've got to write—that's all I can do. I follow a bent. That's writing. It takes all of me to do that. And that's why I'm selfish and cruel and scoundrelly—I know I am and I can't help it" (128).

Feeling worthless and unloved as a person, criticized and unappreciated as a writer who could do nothing else, Caldwell used the novel to trace those patterns which had characterized his life and his writings. For that reason *Love and Money*, from its title through its characters and themes, is an important Caldwell work. It affirms that he himself realized how essentially his dependence upon, and attitudes toward, women had dictated his private life and his writing. In that respect *Love and Money* is as critical to understanding Caldwell's postwar writing career as *The Sacrilege of Alan Kent* is to understanding those forces that made him a writer in the first place.

Writing *Love and Money* may have been cathartic for Caldwell, but during the year he spent agonizing it his dilemmas were not totally resolved. He and June separated and eventually she filed for a divorce which ended their twelve-year marriage in November of 1955. And though Virginia inclined toward marrying Caldwell, she still hesitated. Once she had mentioned how much she enjoyed San Francisco. Shortly after his divorce Caldwell moved there to await her decision. Quietly he signaled his willingness once again to redirect self for the woman's sake.

Yet Caldwell need not have resorted to his usual tactics in this instance. Virginia had come to know him well during the previous five years. She therefore expected nothing more than what he already was when she finally married him on New Year's Day, 1957. Caldwell had now found a mature woman who recognized his needs; she realized that thereafter she would have to accommodate herself to a man whose personal and career demands were all-consuming.

Virginia proved effective in promoting Caldwell's health and in healing the strained relations with his children from his first and third marriages. In the area of his career, however, she could only advise and act as a buffer between Caldwell and those whose criticisms or actions threatened to hurt him. Thus Caldwell persisted in writing novels about women for sixteen more years until his 1973 work, *Annette*, mercifully ended that preoccupation. Virginia, nonetheless, through either direct or more subtle influences, encouraged him to follow other directions in his work. He wrote the children's books *Molly Cottontail* and *The Deer at Our House* in response to her gentle urging. He also turned again to nonfiction, and in such works as *In Search of Bisco*, *Deep South* and *Afternoons in Mid-America* regained some of the critical respect he had earlier squandered.

Whatever the measure, Erskine Caldwell's legacy is a rich one. During the first decade of his career—during the period he was married to Helen—he published quality novels and stories enough to satisfy a lifetime's quota for an average writer. Because he felt he was "special," however, that he had been born with "the gift" to write, such accomplishments were not enough. Even after his priorities and efforts shifted to meet the needs of others, he continued to write as if that were a saving grace necessary for his personal salvation.

That Caldwell could not write himself back to critical redemption should not be cause of censure. Rather, his failed efforts should be respected for what they were—the determined attempts of a man who worked with all his might to honor the storyteller's charge. It is that story—the one he lived—that is ultimately as moving and compelling as any he wrote.

NOTES

[1] "The End of Christy Tucker," "Handy," "The Aggravating Goats" and "My Old Man Hasn't Been the Same Since."

[2] *A Lamp for Nightfall* (1952) had been written in 1931. *Love and Money* (1954) and *Summertime Island* (1969) traded upon personal experience or nostalgia and *The Weather Shelter* (1969) represented Caldwell's notable attempt to explore miscegenation in an almost surrealistic manner.

WORKS CITED

Bourke-White, Margaret. *Portrait of Myself*. New York: Simon, 1963.
Bourke-White, Margaret, Collection. Syracuse U Library, Syracuse, NY.
Caldwell, Caroline Preston. Letter to Erskine Caldwell. 9 Aug. 1937. Bourke-White Collection.
_____. Letter to Helen Caldwell. 3 Sept. 1937. Bourke-White Collection.
_____. Undated marginal notes on letter of inquiry from Robert Cantwell. 23 Aug. 1950. Caldwell Collection, Dartmouth.
Caldwell Collection. Dartmouth College, Baker Library. Hanover, NH.
Caldwell Collection. U of Georgia Library, Athens, GA.
Caldwell Collection. U of Virginia Library, Charlottesville, VA.
Caldwell, Erskine. *Call It Experience*. New York: Duell, 1951.
_____. Letters to the I. S. Caldwells. 6 June 1924. 19 Mar. 1929. 24 Mar. 1930. 2 Oct. 1942. Caldwell Collection, U of Georgia.
_____. Letters to Helen Caldwell. 7 May 1933. 17 June 1933. 12 July 1933. 29 July 1933. 1 Mar. 1937. 22 Apr. 1937. 10 May 1937. Caldwell Collection, Dartmouth.

_____. Letters to Margaret Bourke-White. Feb. 1937 (internally dated). 2 Dec. 1939. 4 Dec. 1939. Bourke-White Collection.

_____. Letter to Atcheson Hench. 26 Apr. 1939. Caldwell Collection, U of Virginia.

_____. Letters to Alfred Morang. 8 Jan. 1943. Alfred Morang Collection. Harvard U Library, Boston, MA.

_____. Letter to June Caldwell. 1 June 1952. Caldwell Collection, U of Virginia.

_____. Letter to Phil Yordan. 21 May 1958. Caldwell Collection, Dartmouth.

_____. *Love and Money*. Boston: Little, 1954; New American Library, Signet, 1960.

_____. *The Sacrilege of Alan Kent*. Portland, ME: Falmouth, 1936.

_____. Statement to June Johnson. 27 Oct. 1942. Caldwell Collection, Dartmouth.

_____. Interview. With Michael Bandry. 20 Aug. 1975. Caldwell Collection, Dartmouth.

Caldwell, Helen. Letter to Erskine Caldwell. 23 Jan. 1938. Bourke-White Collection.

_____ [Helen Caldwell Cushman]. Personal interview. 19-20 July 1978. (See pages 86-97 of this issue for portions of the interview.)

Caldwell, Ira Sylvester. Letter to Erskine Caldwell. Tuesday, Oct. 1939. Bourke-White Collection.

Cowley, Malcolm. *And I Worked at the Writer's Trade*. NewYork: Viking, 1978.

Mair, John. Rev. of *Trouble in July*, by Erskine Caldwell. *New Statesman & Nation* 17 Aug. 1940: 166.

Marshall, Margaret. Rev. of *All Night Long*, by Erskine Caldwell. *Nation* 26 Dec. 1942: 720.

Caldwell at Dartmouth

HENRY TERRIE

The Erskine Caldwell Collection at Dartmouth College (Hanover, New Hampshire), begun in 1940 with the author's gift of typescripts of *God's Little Acre*, *Tobacco Road*, *Southways* and a miscellany of books and magazines, has grown to well over 1,000 volumes of the author's works plus innumerable associated items. It is by a long measure the largest and most comprehensive gathering of Caldwell materials in existence and consequent to the author's death in 1987 will surely become the focal point for research into his life and works. Although Caldwell has been noticed by a great many critics and literary historians through the years, his work still awaits serious and full attention. In the Dartmouth collection prospective students of Caldwell have what may be termed the Caldwell opportunity. My purpose in this essay is to tell the story of the Dartmouth collection, as well as of Caldwell's personal relationship with Dartmouth, to give some account of its contents and to set forth the terms of its public availability.

In 1938 Herbert Faulkner West, a young Professor of Comparative Literature, founded The Friends of the Dartmouth Library, an association devoted to enlarging and improving holdings in the Baker Library at Dartmouth College. In the past half-century The Friends, whose members include bibliophiles from both the alumni body and the general public, have added many valuable materials to the library and today can claim substantial credit for Baker's place among the outstanding research libraries in this country. One of their earliest coups, little more than a year after the group's founding, established Baker as the principal repository for books, papers and memorabilia of Erskine Caldwell.

Late in 1939 Basil O'Connor, a Dartmouth alumnus and chairman of The Friends, persuaded Charles A. Pearce of the publishing house of Duell, Sloan and Pearce to join the group and subsequently put him in touch with Harold Rugg, Associate Librarian of the College. Pearce suggested that Caldwell, then at the peak of his fame as the author of *Tobacco Road* and *God's Little Acre*, might be interested in establishing a collection. In February 1940 Rugg wrote Caldwell, and within a week the bargain was struck. By mid-March the first papers were in hand. Two revealing sidelights emerge from this early correspondence, the first relating to Caldwell's method of composition. When Rugg inquired about handwritten manuscripts, Caldwell's secretary, Rhoda Lynn, replied that Caldwell had never worked in longhand; like the good newspaperman he was, Caldwell composed at the typewriter, a practice which he continued to the end of his career (Lynn to Rugg, 23 Feb. 1940). A second passage illustrates Caldwell's characteristically direct manner. Offering to deposit some unpublished material Caldwell wrote, "My understanding will be, of course, that none of this unpublished material shall be published without my permission, which I do not anticipate giving" (Caldwell to Rugg, 15 Mar. 1940). He never did give that permission.

Through the 1940s Caldwell continued sending books and manuscripts to Dartmouth, and then in 1951 he made the first deposit of personal papers. As in the case of the unpublished fiction, he was very precise about the conditions of use: "1. Certain envelopes will be sealed by me and marked 'This material is not to be published or inspected until 15 years after the death of Erskine Caldwell.' 2. Certain envelopes will be marked 'This material is not to be published or inspected without the consent in writing of Erskine Caldwell, or until after his death.' 3. All other envelopes or material, which will be for the most part clippings, photographs, and manuscripts, will not be restricted as to any use the Library may wish to make of them" (Caldwell to Rugg, 23 Dec. 1951). On these terms the papers were delivered a month later: ten envelopes in the first category, nineteen in the second and five in the third. By this time, of course, the existence of the Dartmouth collection was becoming widely known, and this latest gift was recorded in the *New York Herald Tribune* along with a summary of what was already in place: "Caldwell gifts in the past have included thirty-two proofs, manuscripts, and typescripts; 271 books, of which eighty-three are in foreign languages, eighty anthologies of Mr. Caldwell's short stories and twenty-nine different editions of his famous 'Tobacco Road.' In addition there are twenty-six scrapbooks, largely of clippings relating to his works, a collection of photographs relating to the author and his activities and sixty-four magazines containing first publication of stories by Mr. Caldwell" (25 Mar. 1952).

In November 1961, Caldwell and his wife Virginia began a series of nine official visits to Hanover which transformed his relationship with Dartmouth from one of cordial correspondence to one of warm personal friendship. The occasion was a handsomely arranged exhibit of the collection, a sort of coming-out party for the rich store of materials increasingly envied by other institutions. This brief visit was repeated in September 1962 and October 1966. Then in the fall of 1968 the Caldwells came for a month while Erskine served as Writer-in-Residence. During his residency Caldwell gave a public lecture, visited writing classes and met informally with students and faculty. One especially intriguing by-product of this visit is his handwritten daily diary containing joint observations on life at Dartmouth and on his own current writing. Although he grumbled about having to talk with the college news service ("Trouble is about such interviews—Have only

Caldwell lecturing at Dartmouth College, 1968. Photo courtesy of Dartmouth College Library.

one story of my life and I get bored & short-spoken when once more I have to go through the routine of it''), Caldwell responded fully to the demands made on him, as is clear from the many notes on visits to classes, dormitories and fraternities. Yet at the same time he was determined to remain a writer as well as a resident. Setting out on the first day to give good advice to student writers, he nevertheless resolved to keep at the novel he was writing; and he jotted down for his own benefit some of the advice he was prepared to dispense: ''Every writer must be selfish with his time if he is to accomplish what he sets out to do even though he runs the risk of being called rude and anti-social. If a person cannot take this name-calling, and maintain his dedication to his work, he should take up another trade to find happiness and forget the word business.''

Next morning Caldwell, true to his resolve, was back at the novel-in-progress with a somewhat superstitious comment on naming it: ''Almost ready to decide what the title of this book is to be. So far it is Book #52 but it is far enough along to give it a rightful name. Must be certain, though, because once it is named it can never be anything else.'' Two weeks later it was done, and he recorded an insight into his methods: ''Made final revisions in yellow-paper first draft of novel. Have reached point, which always happens at this stage, when I am willing to let the story (and the writing of it) stand as is. This means I feel I have done the best I can with it—until in a month or so when I'll begin typing final (white paper) MS. And now that this novel has been finished (during the time of being writer-in-residence) I am ready to decide on the final title, THE WEATHER SHELTER. The shelter is a shed on a pony-breeding farm. Not a hut for skiers, not a lodge for hunters, not a refuge for fishermen. And I look for publisher and editor to complain that the title is not precise enough, or sexy enough, or some such reasoning. However, the title will remain as is, because that's what the novel is about'' (Hanover Diary, 14 Oct.- 15 Nov. 1968).

Three years later, at the request of Librarian Edward Connery Lathem, Caldwell agreed to sit for an oil portrait that would become part of the Dartmouth collection, and so in October 1971 he spent a week in the London studio of the late John Gilroy. Apparently Gilroy was not only accustomed to rely heavily on conversation with his subject for revelations of character but also took pride in his skill at the game. In this case, however, he had met his match. From years of exercising the novelist's craft and fending off interviewers, Caldwell had learned how to turn the tables so that *he* was the one who gained insights. Thus Gilroy, somewhat baffled by a sense of depths he could not plumb, was forced to paint an enigmatic surface which gave up no secrets. The countenance portrayed, though strong and lively, is reminiscent of that poker face artfully assumed by many southwestern humorists. The portrait was officially unveiled and presented to Dartmouth during a champagne ceremony attended by the Caldwells in October 1973.

The Caldwells' visits to Hanover continued through the summer of 1980, ranging in length from two or three days to more than a week. The last visit was another significant occasion. During July and August of 1980 Dartmouth, under the aegis of its Montgomery Endowment, invited six novelists to spend a week each on campus for formal and informal meetings including class visits, public lectures and recorded interviews.[1] Each writer was asked to give a lecture or reading and to submit to public grilling by a pair of faculty members. The Caldwell interview, conducted in two hour-long sessions by this writer and colleague A. B. Paulson, covered a broad range of topics. Caldwell spoke on finding and beginning his career, writing as a profession, his lifelong habit of traveling and changing residence, the source and development of ideas for fiction, the mechanics of composition and specific works in his canon.[2] Though the Dartmouth collection contains the texts of at least a dozen other formal interviews given between 1959 and 1986, in addition to many informal ones reported in newspaper articles, the Terrie/Paulson conversations with Caldwell have the added attraction of being available on audio- and video-tape. Except for an unscheduled stopover in 1983 to look at some materials in the Dartmouth files, the 1980 occasion marked the end of Caldwell's appearances at Dartmouth. Nevertheless, both Erskine and Virginia until his death in 1987 and Virginia alone since then have continued to expand the collection in Baker Library. New materials, the contents of a safe-deposit box in Augusta, Maine, were deposited as recently as March 1988.

Even though the collection is still evolving, with new materials arriving and Caldwell's estate caught in legal delays, it is nevertheless possible to give a reasonable account of the holdings that will in time be available to scholars. Dartmouth's on-line catalogue lists for Erskine Caldwell some 1,059 entries, but that number belies the true size of the collection. Many of the catalogue entries refer to sub-collections: for example, the entire set of papers of the Moffett family 1907-1972 (Virginia Moffett Caldwell) is listed as a single entry. Similarly, a single entry appears for seven boxes of magazines containing early stories, one for Caldwell's business papers dated 1933-1938 and one for scrapbooks of newspaper clippings. In addition some items are unlisted, such as the ten envelopes sealed until fifteen years after the author's death and the nineteen envelopes to be unsealed when the Caldwell estate is settled. Precise measurement of the collection, except for its bare physical dimensions (96 linear feet of books, 81 linear feet of manuscripts and 10.5 linear feet of sealed materials), is thus virtually impossible.

First and foremost, the collection contains Caldwell's books themselves. To establish in one place a complete record of Erskine's publications, the Caldwells endeavored to supply over the years a copy of every issue of every one of his works. Barring fugitive printings in obscure locations, they succeeded in providing a complete collection that includes eighty-three copies of *Tobacco Road* in twenty-five languages and fifty-seven copies of *God's Little Acre* in ten languages.[3] There are seventeen stage and screen versions of the fiction. The manuscripts, which are now being catalogued, are really typescripts because Caldwell worked at the keyboard (with two fingers on a series of battered manual typewriters); they do, however, include corrections in the author's hand. These typescripts present the majority of Caldwell's writings, both fiction and nonfiction, as well as miscellaneous papers. Original illustrations, notably some by Hardie Gramatky for *All Night Long* and by Birger Lundquist for *Georgia Boy*, accompany the holdings. Among the various personal papers are numerous letters, some held in the library correspondence files rather than in the Caldwell Collection itself; photographs of both Erskine and Virginia Caldwell; and scrapbooks of newspaper clippings for the years 1931-1967 (the latter now published by University Microfilms). Finally, the collection includes interviews, the most extensive being one of near book length conducted by Jac Tharpe for the Mississippi Oral History Program, and all the known criticism, both published and unpublished, of Caldwell's work.

Although the Dartmouth College library houses by far the most comprehensive gathering of materials relating to Caldwell's life and work, significant collections do exist elsewhere. The largest of these is in the Alderman Library at the University of Virginia. There, in addition to half a dozen manuscripts and a number of photographs and clippings, one may find over 150 letters by and to both Virginia and Erskine: in particular, correspondence with Gordon Lewis, a Charlottesville bookseller; with Mills Lane of the Beehive Press in Savannah, Georgia; with John Cook Wyllie, University librarian; and with Atcheson Hench, Erskine's English teacher at the University. The University of Georgia also has an impressive collection of editions, manuscripts and letters. Smaller collections of material bearing directly or indirectly on Caldwell's career are in university libraries at Nevada Reno, Harvard, Illinois Urbana, Delaware, Syracuse, Columbia and Oregon; in the Library of Congress; in the holdings of the Atlanta Historical Society and the state historical societies of Minnesota and Wisconsin.

Thus, an enormous range of primary and secondary materials for examining the phenomenon of Erskine Caldwell is available—a trove which so far has received minimal attention from scholars and critics. The question of why the author of more than fifty books, whose works have been translated into some forty languages, who may well be the most widely read of all American writers, has been so neglected in his own country, why, in other words, the Caldwell opportunity stands so open, is a subject for another occasion. For the moment one can only say that the materials to repair this neglect are at hand.

NOTES

For gracious and indispensable aid in assembling the materials for this essay and for permission to quote from the Caldwell papers, I wish to thank Edward Connery Lathem, Librarian Emeritus at Dartmouth and Director of the Montgomery Endowment; Margaret Otto, Librarian of the College; Claire Packard, Executive Secretary to the Librarian; Kenneth Cramer, Archivist; and, most particularly, Philip Cronenwett, Special Collections Librarian and Curator of Manuscripts. Ann Southwell, Manuscript Cataloguer at the Alderman Library, very kindly sent me information concerning Caldwell materials at the University of Virginia. And a special note of thanks to Virginia Caldwell, whose friendship, along with that of her late husband, I have treasured for many years.

[1] The other writers invited were Wallace Stegner, John Cheever, Robert Penn Warren, Bernard Malamud and John Updike.

[2] Other topics Caldwell addressed included his preference for Webster's Second over the Third, his use of plain style, readers vs. critics, "pan" and "fan" mail, profanity and pornography, censorship, the nature and use of experience in writing, the relation between comedy and tragedy and between history and fiction.

[3] Over all there are printings of Caldwell's work in at least thirty-nine languages, though only a sure knowledge of the many Slavic languages and dialects could guarantee the accuracy of these counts.

Caldwell in Japan

FUJISATO KITAJIMA

Erskine Caldwell published some sixty-four books during his lifetime, including twenty-five novels, twelve works of nonfiction, two children's books and four picture-texts with Margaret Bourke-White. He published one-hundred-twenty-eight short stories. His work often portrayed impoverished and ignorant share-croppers struggling for survival in the period of the Great Depression. Like James Farrell or John Steinbeck, he was initially regarded primarily as a social novelist. The critical period of the Depression not only gave his novels social significance but also rendered them fashionable in the thirties and consequently out of date today. If Caldwell's fiction was indeed too contingent upon special circumstances, and if the author failed to touch a universal note, failed to treat things that are fundamental and permanent to humanity, then it is no wonder he would be forgotten as times change.

I do not think that Caldwell was simply a writer of his time, however, and I do not understand why he has not enjoyed a better reputation in America, why Americans have not treated him with seriousness. It occurs to me that Americans, especially southerners, may object to Caldwell's picture of America or of the South. They complain that Caldwell's work is a distortion of reality and gives a false impression. Indeed, when I began to read Caldwell's books in the middle of the 1950s in my college days in Tokyo, one of my American professors advised me not to do so, adding that Caldwell's work misrepresented his country.

But it is important to remember that when William Faulkner made his famous list of the five greatest contemporary American novelists, he ranked Caldwell in fourth place, behind Wolfe, Faulkner himself and John Dos Passos, but ahead of Ernest Hemingway ("Interview" 225). Also, when Faulkner visited Japan in August 1955 to participate in the Nagano Seminar, he said of Caldwell's work, "For plain, simple style, it's first rate. There was a thought or a certain moving power and quality in his first book, *Tobacco Road*" (Jelliffe 57-58). As James Korges notes in his seminal pamphlet on Caldwell, "When a writer of a complex, involuted, rich, moving, powerful prose, like Faulkner's, goes out of his way to praise a lean, spare, direct, plain style, like Caldwell's, we do well to pay attention" (6).

It is hard for us Japanese today to appreciate the gigantic impact of *Tobacco Road*, with its angry picture of oppressed Georgia sharecroppers, bursting like a storm over Depression America. But I think it is very important, although difficult, to explain Caldwell's popularity in Japan and to describe when and how it occurred. In May 1932 Caldwell's short story "The Empty Room" was translated by Azuma Kondo in a small literary magazine *Shin Eibungaku Kenyu* (*New Studies in English Literature*), edited by Sei Ito. The date was a year before Viking published *We Are the Living*, so it seems that the Japanese version was translated from the Autumn 1931 issue of *Pagany*, in which it first appeared. In 1937 *Tobacco Road*, with the author's "Preface" to Japanese readers, was translated by Komatsu Kitamura, and in 1940 *American Earth* was translated by Takashi Sugiki. Another important scholar who introduced Caldwell to Japan was Professor Masami Nishikawa, who, as early as the 1940s, translated Caldwell's early works and short stories in *Eigo Seinen* (*The Rising Generation*) and other literary magazines and who read with his students *Kneel to the Rising Sun* and other stories by Caldwell, along with works by Henry James, Ambrose Bierce, John Steinbeck, Ernest Hemingway and William Faulkner.

During the war itself and the following few terrible postwar years, most Japanese were forced to devote themselves entirely to the one question of staying alive. Little literature of importance was published in Japan in those years. Certain influential left-wing writers who had been prisoners of war or exiled in Siberia or in the Philippines repatriated to Japan to write memoirs, including works about cannibalism and the darker side of human nature. Their books, together with translations of contemporary foreign works, mostly American, took up a large part of the bestseller lists. Detective stories, new types of escapist literature, and pornographic novels vitiating public morals in the chaos of postwar society began to be published, reflecting the low standards of the reading public at that time. Some magazine publishers were obliged to put a blonde nude figure on the cover of each monthly issue so that it would sell, and to disguise even the serious short stories with titles of a vaguely improper nature. Such was the chaotic phase of postwar fiction.

Also right after World War II, American GIs of the Occupation Army who flooded Japan liked to read Caldwell's books in paperback editions. Like Johnny Appleseeds, they planted Caldwellian seeds in Japanese earth.[1] Because of their covers and their supposed subject matter, Caldwell's books became very popular in Japan. In the 1950s, Naotaro Tatsunokuchi, Shunji Shimizu and other scholars translated with enthusiasm as many as 30 books by Caldwell, including *Tragic Ground* (1950), *Journeyman* (1950), *God's Little Acre* (1952), *Trouble in July* (1953), *The Sure Hand of God* (1953), *Love and Money* (1955), *Gretta* (1956), *Claudelle Inglish* (1959), *A House in the Uplands* (1959) and *This Very Earth* (1959). *Georgia Boy* was translated by Taishiro Shirai as *Nanbu Katagi* (*Southern Traits*) in 1955, and *Gulf Coast Stories* was published in 1958. By my count, 16

Caldwell on his first visit to Japan in 1960. He is seated between Professor Naotaro Tatsunokuchi and Virginia Caldwell. Photo courtesy of Dartmouth College Library.

novels and 95 short stories by Caldwell, in addition to 3 nonfiction books—*Some American People* (1953), *Call It Experience* (1965) and *In Search of Bisco* (1973)—have been translated into Japanese. Still more, 125 essays by both Japanese scholars and academic critics were written and more than 60 inexpensive reprints with introduction, translation or notes for Japanese college students were published. Even in English textbooks published for Japanese high school students and approved by the Ministry of Education one can today find Caldwell stories like "Molly Cottontail," "The Strawberry Season," "The Lonely Day," "Crown-Fire" and "Vick Shore and the Good of the Game."

It must be said that Caldwell has not had consistently good translators in Japan as have other American writers, such as Hemingway, Faulkner, Steinbeck and Fitzgerald. Among the best, however, are Nozomu Konno (*Gretta*, 1956), Yutaka Shimizu, Hajime Imai, Seiya Nishi, Kaname Imanaga (*A House in the Uplands* and *This Very Earth*, 1959; *The Bastard* and *Poor Fool*, 1962), Miyoko Aomi and Osamu Kato. Professor Kato also translated twelve English articles on Caldwell, *Selected Critical Essays on E. Caldwell* (1977). He and I are now preparing another collection of essays, mainly on Caldwell's short stories. Perhaps most honored of Caldwell's translators was Professor Nishikawa (1904-1988), mentioned above, who was also a great scholar and teacher. He and Caldwell died within a year of each other. Professor Nozomu Konno was one of Nishikawa's students, and Konno borrowed several precious books from him when he wrote his important study *Caldwell: Hito to Sakuhin* (*Caldwell: The Man and His Works*) in 1962, seven years before James Korges published his significant work in America. Though it was an introductory book with 172 pages, it is a landmark, both because it was the first book of critical studies of Caldwell in the world and because of its superb academic content. Nishikawa-sensei translated both novels and short stories by Bierce, Steinbeck, Faulkner, Maugham and others, but he never translated a novel by Caldwell. He did, however, publish two annotated editions of *Kneel to the Rising Sun, & Other Stories* (1955) and *Georgia Boy* (1966) from Kenkyusha LTD., both of which sell well even today.

Erskine Caldwell came to Japan in February 1960, in November 1971 and in April 1982. On his first trip he announced to the gathered press at Tokyo International Airport, "I have assured various Japanese intellectuals that I'm not over here gathering material for a Japanese *Tobacco Road* or a Buddha's Little Acre." He jokingly told the newsmen that he had come to Japan because Asian flu was rampant in the U. S. and he felt it was better to catch the disease in its native place if he were to catch it at all. Asked which of his books he liked best, he answered, "My next one" *(Sankei)*. Caldwell's remarks introduced us to his impish sense of humor.

Caldwell revisited Japan in 1971 in connection with the United States Information Service, which had arranged a program of seminars and talks before Japanese college students. On 19 November he spoke before an informal group of professors of English literature and journalists at the American Cultural Center in Akasaka, Tokyo. Among his comments were the following:

> I am a practitioner of the story in print. I'm finished with short stories, and I want to write stories of great expanse. (Kenrick)

> My work consists of words. I'm a storyteller. I have spent my life writing stories as I find them in life. I try to delineate, elucidate, specify what people do, what people say, how people live. I'm just an ordinary person. I talk about the simple things of life. Everything else I leave to the scholars, the philosophers, the psychologists. My only interest is to tell stories of live people and write what they do, no matter whether I approve of them or not. (Yoshii)

> I have written one book a year for the last fifty years and maybe one hundred and fifty short stories published in magazines and books. To me, fiction is the real heart of writing. I think I am a romanticist, though others say I am too realistic, too hard. The purpose of all the books of ficiton I have written is to provide a mirror into which people may look. Whatever good or harm my books do depends on an individual's reaction to the image he sees in the mirror. (Yoshii)

Fifty or more professors and journalists attended this discussion and reception at the American Center, which lasted almost five hours. Caldwell became hoarse and seemingly weary and guarded in his talk about his fictional themes and methods.

When Caldwell came to Japan in 1982 to attend the inaugural ceremony of the Erskine Caldwell Literary Society and to be the guest at a banquet in a Tokyo hotel for members of the Society, he had lost half of both lungs in two operations for cancer. He was slightly bent, a bit feeble, but not broken under the weight of his eighty years. He looked like a man who had spent many years leaning into unfavorable winds—the winds of criticism, the winds of censorship and now the winds of neglect. The trip included no plans for a round-table discussion before the large gathering because of traditional Japanese consideration for the old and sick. This was to have been a private trip, undisturbed by journalists or others. I, as a friend and interpreter, was privileged to stay with Caldwell in a Tokyo hotel for an entire week. Still fresh in my memory is his impromptu tale told at a luncheon party to his Japanese friends and publishers as a "thank you for this wonderful lunch." The tale concerned an automobile salesman in Detroit dealing in Cadillacs, Lincolns and other large luxury limousines. The advances of Japanese minicars, coupled with a gasoline shortage, had made it difficult for him to keep going. The only way out was for the salesman to commit suicide. He bought a "suicide pill" at a drugstore. After taking the pill, he fell fast asleep and had a dream. A genie appeared in his dream and told him that he would grant him one wish before his death. The salesman rejoiced. He asked the genie to make him a salesman dealing in imported cars in a large city where he had many customers. The genie agreed to grant him his wish. A moment later, the salesman woke up and found himself in Tokyo. As he wished, he had many imported cars to sell— Cadillacs and Lincolns!

Looking out the window at the forest of high-rise buildings in the heart of Tokyo, Caldwell added, as if whispering, "Today the poor salesman is going around Tokyo, trying to sell Cadillacs and Lincolns." What enchanted us most was his great eloquence as he told the story. Speaking in a thick, heavy voice and with the slow drawl characteristic of southern American English, he paused here and there as if he were trying to learn our reactions to the story. The pauses enhanced his narrative, especially the effect of the ending. To us his narrative was perfect. It afforded a vivid glimpse into the fine craftsmanship of Caldwell, a first-class storyteller.

Although Japan is so strikingly different from other countries in many aspects of its culture, Japanese people have always taken an avid interest in the literary and artistic trends of the outside world, especially since the latter half of the nineteenth century. Erskine Caldwell is one nonJapanese writer whose works are very familiar to Japanese readers. His mastery of a style similar to that of Ernest Hemingway has appealed strongly to the Japanese reading public as well as to young Japanese writers. The ease with which Caldwell seemed to have written his short stories and novels did not mean that there had been no deliberate effort, neither did the simplicity necessarily mean no complexity and depth underneath. Caldwell always kept in mind a preference for compact and brief statements in simple sentence structures. He tried to avoid compound or complex sentences and thus relied much more upon participial constructions as a means to achieve brevity of statement. The flat and simple colloquial style was well considered by the Japanese reader for both its primitivistic power and its effective display of humor. It is true that the author's humor was often hampered by the intrusion of violence and sometimes turned into pathos or even callousness, but it nevertheless continued to drift everywhere throughout his work, much like subterranean water.

Caldwell's humor probably derived from American tall tales or folklore of both the legendary, peddling Yankees and the irrepressible backwoodsmen. As Henry S. Canby said, "Caldwell is Mark Twain's spiritual heir" (xi). But his tall tales are also somewhat similar to Japanese folklore. Indeed, *God's Little Acre* reads like some sort of homemade mythology: the Waldens are reminiscent of the tribal period with great patriarchs. Another book which greatly appeals to our readers is the perfectly delightful *Georgia Boy*, a masterpiece of humor in which Caldwell has woven comedy and irony, exaggeration and eloquence, totally unexpected ideas and amazing behavior. It is not surprising that Japanese college students, especially female students, love reading Caldwell in English.

Virginia Caldwell once wrote me, "He didn't have much peace in life, it was always a struggle and even though he declared that the critics didn't bother him I know that as sensitive as he was, all of the banning and anger in the beginning must have been very hard for him to bear. He was so young when it all began, young and naive about so many things." The prominent Japanese novelist Ken Kaiko said of Caldwell, "This man with broad shoulders and long legs wandered through the American continent, spending his time freely working, watching and writing. Even after he gained fame, he refused to sit nice and cozy on it. He yearned for odyssey without reward. He strove constantly to keep himself hungry for people and life itself."

NOTES

[1] I have one copy: *Stories by Erskine Caldwell [A Wartime Book]*, published by Duell, Sloan & Pearce, 1944.

WORKS CITED

Faulkner, William. "Interview with Cynthia Grenier." Ed. James B. Meriwether and Michael Millgate. *Lion in the Garden: Interviews with William Faulkner 1926-1962*. New York: Random, 1968. 215-27.
Caldwell, Virginia. Letter to the author. 15 July 1988.

48   *Caldwell in Japan*

Canby, Henry Seidel. "Introduction." *The Pocket Book of Erskine Caldwell*. New York: Pocket Books, 1947: vii-xvi. (Reprinted in *Critical Essays on Erskine Caldwell*. Ed. Scott MacDonald. Boston: G. K. Hall, 1981. 214-20.)

Jelliffe, Robert A., ed. *Faulkner at Nagano*. Tokyo: Kenkyusha, 1956.

Kaiko, Ken. Jacket notes. Trans. Fujisato Kitajima. *Sakka to Naru Ho [Call it Experience]*. By Erskine Caldwell. Trans. Yuji Tanaka. Tokyo: Shiseido, 1965.

Kenrick, Vivienne. "Personality Profile: Erskine Caldwell." *Japan Times* [Tokyo] 29 Nov. 1971: 6.

Kondo, Azuma, trans. "The Empty Room." By Erskine Caldwell. Ed. Sei Ito. *Shin Eibungaku Kenyu [New Studies in English Literature]* 6 (May 1932): 253-58.

Korges, James. *Erskine Caldwell*. U of Minnesota Pamphlets on American Writers No. 78. Minneapolis: U of Minnesota P, 1969.

Sankei Shinbun [Tokyo] 2 Feb. 1960, evening ed.: 4.

Yoshii, Michiko. "No More Short Stories for Me." *Daily Yomiuri* [Tokyo] 28 Nov. 1971: 6.

SELECTED WORKS ON CALDWELL IN JAPAN

Imai, Koh. "The Humor of Erskine Caldwell." *Gunma Journal of Liberal Arts and Science* 2 (1968): 75-83.

Imanage, Kaname. "Oedipus Complex of Erskine Caldwell." *Bodai Kiyo* 5 (1960): 1-20.

_____. "Erskine Caldwell as a Spokesman for Negroes." *Bodai Kiyo* 12 (1966): 105-25.

_____. "The Style of Erskine Caldwell." *Bodai Kiyo* 19 (1970): 551-61.

Kitajima, Fujisato. "An Essay on *Trouble in July*." *Chuo-Eibei-Bungaku* 7 (1973): 36-49.

_____. "Erskine Caldwell and Margaret Bourke-White's Four Picture-Texts." *Chuo-Eibei-Bungaku* 13 (1979): 87-98.

_____. "Erskine Caldwell's Home in Deep South." *Chuo-Eibei-Bungaku* 15 (1981): 56-70.

_____. *Erskine Caldwell: A Bibliography in Japan (1932-1981)*. *Kenkyu Kiyo* 3 (14 Apr. 1982): 1-36.

_____. "Erskine Caldwell, A Chronology (1903-1985)." *Kenkyu Kiyo* 7 (31 Mar. 1986): 15-41.

_____. "Horo no Nanbu Sakka: Erskine Caldwell (Erskine Caldwell: A Wandering Southern Writer)." *The Rising Generation* CXXXIII (1 July 1987): 184-86.

_____. "Farewell, Georgia Boy—In Memory of Mr. Erskine P. Caldwell." *Kenkyu Kiyo* 9 (31 Mar. 1988): 37-76.

Konno, Nozomu. *Caldwell: Hito to Sakuhin*. Tokyo: Nan'undo, 1962.

Tochiyama, Michiko. "Homage to Caldwell: A Study of *God's Little Acre*." *Gendai Eigo Bungaku Kenkyu* 2: 1-18.

Caldwell's Fiction: Growing Towards Trash?

SYLVIA J. COOK

If there has been any critical consensus about Erskine Caldwell's long career as a fiction writer among his admirers and disparagers alike, it is that there was a definite change in the nature of his work by the mid-1940s, at a time of some consequence in his life. It came at the culmination of his international travels and reporting with Margaret Bourke-White and his corresponding detachment from his literary native ground in the South, and was also coincidental with his achievement of fame, financial success, access to enormous reading audiences, and a marked change in literary bedfellows from those of his early years. Then he had scrutinized the work of his fellow contributors to experimental, modernist and radical magazines such as *transition, Hound and Horn, Contact* and *The New Masses,* looking for what was vital, honest and new in the fiction of the early 1930s. Now, after a decade of innovation on his own part in novels, short stories and nonfiction, he dwelt in the relative isolation of his achievement and the security of publishers' contracts. In broader social terms, the change in Caldwell's work came after the end of the Depression and the left-wing political fiction it had helped nurture, while in the most specific context of Caldwell's fiction, it came about midway through his projected ten-novel cyclorama of the South, after *Tobacco Road* (1932), *God's Little Acre* (1933), *Journeyman* (1935), and *Trouble in July* (1940). The change was most succinctly characterized in Faulkner's dispassionate verdict on Caldwell's work after his early fiction: "It gradually grew towards trash, I thought" (58). Other commentators have been less laconic than Faulkner in both their censure and analysis of Caldwell's later fiction, but, although there are some, like C. Hugh Holman and James Korges, who have found merit in it, in general the response has been disappointment, frustration and ultimate neglect.

Among those critics who had, from the outset, been most skeptical of Caldwell's literary motives, the change in his work in the 1940s was seen merely as an intensification and acceleration of his most suspect qualities. He was, as Jonathan Daniels put it in a review of *Tragic Ground* (1944), seeking "pay-dirt" by mining the lower depths of American life for sensationalism, sexual titillation and horror, all under the convenient disguise of social and political exposé and reform (46). Lon Tinkle, in discussing "the distressing nose dive" in Caldwell's talent in *A House in the Uplands* (1946) and *The Sure Hand of God* (1947), felt that

Caldwell had moved from artistic detachment to indifference to his characters (12); Harrison Smith argued that, by 1946, Caldwell had exhausted his stereotypes and "come to the end of his rope" (8) and *Time* confidently announced "Caldwell's Collapse" in 1948, arguing that he had been misled by "party-line critics and earnest sociologists" into taking his sordid stories too seriously (82). Carl Bode, looking back from 1955 at Caldwell's early successes, proposed bluntly that "sex did the job" (358), and suggested that he exploited this element even more in the postwar years, when social significance was no longer fashionable. Behind all these critiques was the clear innuendo that Caldwell had used up whatever original talent he might have had but was continuing to exploit that vein in his writing best guaranteed to bring him large popular audiences and good financial returns.

Even among Caldwell's more sympathetic critics, however, who refrained from impugning his motives, there was a widespread awareness of changes in both the direction and quality of his fiction during the 1940s. James Korges considered that the short-story cycle *Georgia Boy* (1943) marked a division between the first part of Caldwell's southern cyclorama and the second, in which the author "seemed to have difficulty in getting back into his fictional world and in creating wholly satisfying books" (44). Malcolm Cowley felt that, in the last six novels of the cyclorama, Caldwell began to substitute "extensity for intensity, at the risk of exhausting his material" (128). And Harvey Klevar found that, after the 1930s, Caldwell's fiction lost what he called "its cosmically sustaining vitality" and that "by the early Forties Caldwell had undergone some changes which must have essentially affected his fictional attitude" (75). Korges noted, however, not a desire to pander to public tastes for violence and salaciousness but, rather, a tendency towards increased didacticism and a diminution of the grotesque mixture of humor and horror that characterized Caldwell's best early work (42). Cowley saw Caldwell's "'earthy, robust' country humor" being replaced by "kinky urban humor" (130), and Klevar argued that his early trancendentalism was now transformed into humanism as he focused on increasingly sophisticated modern people (74). Cowley attempted to explain the alteration in Caldwell's fiction as a direct consequence of the author's determination to preserve himself in isolation from all previous and contemporary literature and his consequent failure to learn, to grow and to make sufficient demands on his innate storytelling gift (125, 127). Margaret Bourke-White, Caldwell's wife from 1939 to 1942, gave an even simpler explanation for the seeming enervation of Caldwell's talent in the 1940s, even as his pace of publication increased. She wrote in her autobiography: "Erskine had a favorite saying which he repeated very often—so often that I think he convinced himself of its truth. 'The life of a writer is just ten years,' he would say" (196).

Caldwell himself, however, never publicly acceded to any theory of decline or change in his work and, as late as 1986, seemed to take a certain perverse pleasure in ranking *Tragic Ground* (1944), *A House in the Uplands* (1946), *Episode in Palmetto* (1950), *Gretta* (1955) and *Summertime Island* (1968) as among his most interesting works (Arnold, 294)—certainly an unconventional selection from *any* critical perspective. He did, in other contexts, certainly acknowledge the vicissitudes of his reputation and offer some indirect explanations of them that are relevant to a change in direction in his work. He reflected several times in *Writing in America* his belief that works of literature, including his own, were intimately tied, in both content and reception, to the contexts in which they appeared. This seemed to him especially true of that new American literature that had begun in the 1930s, in an era of "despair and despondency," when "a new generation of native writers" allowed Americans to see "their lives in true perspective" (116). He insisted further, in an interview, "Fiction in America changes almost from one day to the next. We are still a very volatile civilization. . . .In America, fiction reflects current lifestyles, economic conditions, wars, lots of things. The interests of American readers change with the times. Especially here, writing has to be contemporary" (Broadwell 152). There is certainly an implicit admission here that Caldwell felt the need to keep his fiction apace with a kinetic society and thence that any new era, such as that after the Depression and World War II, would require novels commensurate with its concerns.

When he returned to the United States, after his arduous wartime reporting in the Soviet Union, Caldwell was clearly ready to resume fiction writing and take up his unfinished cyclorama series. He had satisfied, perhaps sated, for some time to come, his desire to write nonfiction. He had, with the publication of *Jackpot* in 1940, reached the goal of one hundred short stories that he had set himself at the beginning of his career. The southern cyclorama remained to be pursued, but now in a context very different both in fact and in Caldwell's imaginative rendering of it, from that which had dominated his earlier novels. It was, as Cowley suggested, more extensive historically, geographically and socially than that of the early novels, and after the cyclorama was completed in 1950, Caldwell moved completely outside his shaping southern environment and into his own version of the modern, dislocated, urban world. Though he reverted often to southern settings in the twelve remaining novels he published between 1950 and 1973, he did not recapture along with them enough of his early reputation to win any general retraction of *Time*'s cruel epitaph for him in 1948 as the literary equivalent of "a once-talented dancer who still remembers all the steps and postures but has forgotten how to dance" (84).

Those works in which Caldwell metaphorically "danced" have come, by general critical consent, to include not only the first four cyclorama novels but also the short-story collections *American Earth* (1931), *We Are the Living* (1933), *Kneel to the Rising Sun* (1935), *Southways* (1938) and the cycle of linked stories,

Georgia Boy (1943). Together these constitute the body of work he was accused of parodying and exploiting, or alternatively, falling away from in his later career. Despite the leveling "hookworm" stereotype later applied to them (Smith 8), these works of fiction are widely varied in themes, imagery and characters, although they display in common a distinctive and pervasive intellectual and artistic vision of the world. This vision is most simply suggested in a phrase Caldwell used on a number of occasions to describe what he found most intriguing about his fellow humans, namely their "antics and motivations" (*Writing in America*, Introduction). The word "antics" suggests behavior that is irrational, unpredictable and comic, while "motivations" implies the scientific and deterministic origins of people's conduct. For Caldwell, there was never any fixed balance between the explicable and the inexplicable but rather a constantly shifting emphasis among different kinds of causality—political, environmental, historical— and the possibility of no causality at all beyond whim and accident. Caldwell's people might thus be depicted as acting out of perverse impulse or innate depravity, out of their own foolish misunderstandings, or the consequences of hunger, disease, violence and degradation inflicted on them by others. One of the great achievements of this fiction was in Caldwell's ability simultaneously to insist on the absurd and incorrigible aspects of the human condition and on the urgent need to correct inequity, misery and exploitation that arose from defects in human society. His fiction, though often accused of reducing people to the level of animals, was in fact concerned with precisely those obsessions, spiritual yearnings, quirks and contradictions that separated his characters from merely instinctual nature, although he certainly did not hesitate to explore the working of those instincts. He was fascinated by the perpetual struggles for ascendancy among classes, races, sexes and individuals and bemused by the frequency with which conventional wisdom about the outcome might be thwarted by human perversity. Such a theoretical view of the world was most aptly realized in a literary style that was at once both simple and oblique, grossly naturalistic and comically grotesque. In the first four novels of the cyclorama and the early short-story collections, Caldwell arrived at a dissonant style, a remote setting and the central metaphorical figure of the poor white—images so perfectly integral to his vision that it was only later, when he sought new settings and images, that their soundness was fully apparent.

Before he came to this assured style in the 1930s, Caldwell had experimented in two earlier novels, *The Bastard* (1929) and *Poor Fool* (1930), and in the prose poem *The Sacrilege of Alan Kent* (1931), with the literary methods of verisimilitude and surrealism in anonymous urban underworlds and mythical rural settings, and he had rehearsed a wide range of narrative sensibilities from hardboiled to poetic. When he came to write *Tobacco Road*, he viewed this excursion into the southern world of his childhood as a means of exorcising the ghost of his past before moving on to other concerns (*Call It Experience* 101, 103). Like many such childhood ghosts, however, the memory of remote and impoverished southern communities became the animating spirit of much of his ensuing fiction. It provided him with a link to the larger social and economic concerns of Depression America and with an intimately familiar setting that allowed him both to control and intensify his incongruous depictions of human nature. This context permitted him to explore most thoroughly the character and predicament of the southern poor white who was already, in both literary and social tradition, a fusion of contradictory and dissonant qualities, comic and pathetic, abused and intractable, lazy and violent, cunning and naive. Firmly rooted in history and society, indeed festering there, the poor whites were nevertheless inherently perplexing in their material dilemma and spiritual nature, and thus, for Caldwell, were as superb a metaphor for his fictional inquiries as the New England Puritans were for Hawthorne. The wry, dispassionate prose in which he described their shame and suffering as well as their quaint and ludicrous ways brought accusations of callousness from reviewers and critics who wished to indulge in more predictable responses of anger and pity and were bewildered by Caldwell's juxtapositions of starving women, like Ada Lester, who worried about the correct length of the hemline of their burial dresses, or harelipped, hungry girls whose strongest appetite was lust. Other critics, who wished to relish Caldwell's earthy comedy, found themselves disconcerted by reminders of the disease, deformity and suffering of the participants and rejected his naturalism as an intrusion of left-wing didacticism into robust folklore. Caldwell's detachment, however, was not the product of indifference (as his simultaneous nonfiction powerfully demonstrated) nor of any narrow political agenda other than the sense that poverty was a token neither of the worthiness nor the moral failure of the poor. Instead, Caldwell found among the poor whites the artistic possibilities for bringing extreme physical, emotional and spiritual conditions into dramatic juxtaposition and for creating a hermetic, imaginary and self-contained universe that burlesqued the real one, but contained—especially during the Depression—enough echoes of urgent social problems to prevent its dismissal as politically and morally irrelevant to the national crisis.

The first cyclorama novels and short stories show on Caldwell's part a daring combination of surreal imagery and social allegory, of caricatures and symbolic events that emanate from his grotesque subjects. *Trouble in July*, for example, concludes with two mob murders of a black man and a white woman which are jointly credible as effective symbols only in the cohesive extravagance of the imaginary world of Andrewjones, where enormity is the norm and every incident bears an allegorical weight. In the context of the cotton mill strike in *God's Little Acre*, the girls with eyes like morning glories who kiss the mill walls are as defiantly fantastic as Will Thompson's shredding of Griselda's clothes into minute particles of lint such as the workers will once again weave when they take control of the power in the mill. Caldwell is able to evoke his characters' dreams and obsessions on both a grand and foolish scale, such as befits their ambiguous status, from Jeeter Lester's agrarian dreams and turnip theft in *Tobacco Road* to the efforts of three drunk men in *Journeyman* to peer through a hole in a barn wall and seek eternity on the other side. In the short stories deliberately disturbing images and incidents abound: in "Saturday Afternoon" Tom Denny, a butcher by both trade and preference, sleeps with his head on a hunk of raw steak; in "The Growing Season" a heat-crazed cotton farmer slaughters an ominously unidentified victim to placate the savage climate; in "Blue Boy" a retarded black youth is forced to entertain a group of white men with a display of his deformities. These are all regional caricatures, embellished and adapted to their creator's enquiry into the mysteries of human conduct. The distortions, twists and surprises of Caldwell's confounded poor white universe were extended in his early works to characters with less malleable stereotypes, so that the poor white mode became a way of viewing a broader group than that suggested by the term itself. Caldwell at first depicted blacks as both publicly prevaricating victims and secret and taunting rivals of whites: they were gargantuan heroes like Candy-Man Beechum; eccentrics like Dose Muffin, who, on one epic occasion, had chased a fly across the countryside for eight days; and dupes like Youster Brown, with his purchase of nine dollars worth of mumble. They were lovers and fools, people of conscience and greedy cowards. Caldwell's women too were at first part of this comprehensively incongruous sense of human nature: they were lascivious preachers with grotesque physical deformities, starving girls driven into both willing and unwilling prostitution, and bored wives seducing strangers while their husbands slept. He carefully noted the economic suffering of the poor, the injustices of society toward blacks, and the entrapment of women, but always in conjunction with this clearly imaginary and extravagant mode. The early works produced some curious efforts on the part of Congressional representatives and members of the press to deny or vindicate the factual basis of Caldwell's fiction, but although Georgia's numbers of clayeaters, harelips and lynch mobs were scrutinized and argued over, this was merely an extension of a similar critical tendency to focus on one element in a paradoxical vision rather than to admit the disconcerting effect of the yoking.

By the time he published *Trouble in July* in 1940, Caldwell had completed four novels based on the intricate intermingling of deprivation and depravity in this extended poor white population. He had examined the predisposition of his people to lust, religious ecstasy and violence and had exposed the debasement and boredom that were the products of inequity and poverty. When he returned to the cyclorama with *Tragic Ground* in 1944, he made an immediate effort to deal with a more contemporary and visible version of poor white social problems by setting the novel among uprooted rural people who had been lured from their land during the war to work in urban munitions plants. The novel depicts both the degenerate lives of its victims and their duplicity in rejecting and exploiting their new world. Caldwell directs a good deal of irony in this novel to professional social workers in the community who talk reductively of the "complex patterns of modern life" and of people's "maladjustment to reality" (63) when, in fact, Spence Douthit, the novel's protagonist, seems the logical and ugly product of a complete adjustment to that world's reality. Despite his satire of the social workers' pat theories and pretentious jargon, however, Caldwell himself shows an increasing tendency in this and later novels to look to the formulaic terms of sociology and psychology for explanations of his characters' predicaments, and to label what was formerly inscrutable in his characters' behavior "complexes," "hang-ups" and "break-downs." Allied to this increased emphasis on a rather narrow brand of determinism is a gradual simplification of the people themselves into more obviously innocent or culpable, pathetic or unwholesome types, and indeed a simplification of whole novels, created in the mold of social comedies, melodramas or thrillers rather than the incongruous commingling of genres that had formerly taxed Caldwell's reviewers into coinages like "absurd naturalism," "grim comedy" or "tragic farce" in order to suggest their perplexing quality. Caldwell had, since his earliest publications, expressed a good deal of frustration with his readers and critics for their failure to understand the meaning of his work. This feeling rapidly evolved into bitter vituperative against critics and, in the later novels of the cyclorama and afterwards, an increasing tendency to spell out in bluntly naturalistic terms his meanings and morals, without the complicating contexts of strangeness and unpredictability that marked the earlier work. This tendency, in conjunction with a concern for topicality, was most immediately manifest in the altered fictional world of the later cyclorama novels.

The settings of these novels display a general movement from rural to urban, from containment and stasis to uprooting and change and from a hazy timelessness to a more precise contemporaneity. It is true that the settings of the first novels were neither exclusively rural nor isolated from topical concerns, but they nevertheless belong to a vision of human affairs that is self-contained, coherent and internally quite consistent. There is no disjunction between the grotesque characters and their grotesque environment, no confusion—on Caldwell's part at least—about the exact distance at which they exist from contemporary social, political and psychological facts. As Caldwell's fictional world gradually became something more akin to a radically reduced model of our own, however, his ingenuous narratives, outrageous dialogue and ritual repetition became increasingly inappropriate to its authenticity. He maintained in an interview late in life that he believed the poor white mentality lived on in the South long after the material circumstances of the poor white had disappeared (Arnold 211), but any effort in his fiction to separate the twisted spirit from the physical context of the poor white struck at his richest and most effective metaphor.

In his 1946 novel, *A House in the Uplands*, he attempted a reversal of class stereotypes, with the upper-class Grady Dunbar revealing all the degenerate qualities he accused his own white tenants of possessing while the tenants acted with restraint and decency, but the resulting novel is merely melodramatic and tendentious. Likewise, when he tried to endow the middle-class heroines of *Episode in Palmetto* and *Gretta* with the peculiar sexual appetites of his early poor white women, the result was a psychological case study in aberrant behavior rather than a symbol of sublime yearnings trapped in carnality. Similarly, as Caldwell moved away from his poor whites, the obsessions and longings of his characters diminished in significance, from Jeeter Lester's agrarian fantasies in *Tobacco Road* to Chism Crockett's thwarted ambition to be a storekeeper in *This Very Earth*. Even Caldwell's black characters seem affected by the reduction of his poor whites. There are no longer types like Handsome Brown in *Georgia Boy* who likes to loaf and speculate, or larger-than-life folk heroes like Candy-Man Beechum, but instead prudent, educated, conscientious and lust-free blacks, who may well serve the moral purpose of reversing ugly stereotypes but who are also, in James Devlin's phrase, ''neutered paragons'' (96). Caldwell did not suddenly stop writing about poor whites after the 1930s—far from it—but he ventured increasingly out of the fictional territory they had inhabited, sometimes retaining southern settings but exploring different social classes (as in *A House in the Uplands* and *Episode in Palmetto*); sometimes retaining physical poverty as a characteristic but moving the poor into urban settings (as in *Tragic Ground*); or (as in Chism Crockett in *This Very Earth*) retaining a kind of poor white mentality without either poverty or a remote rural environment.

In Caldwell's depiction of women the change was most marked. This was a subject of increasing interest to him, and both the short-story collections *Gulf Coast Stories* (1956) and *Certain Women* (1957) and the novels *Gretta* (1955) and *Claudelle Inglish* (1958) are devoted to the lives and dilemmas of women. These two latter novels have indeed almost identical concerns, their main difference being that *Gretta* has an anonymous and unspecified urban setting and a middle-class heroine while *Claudelle Inglish* returns to a poor family in a small southern town. Both novels explore the peculiar sexual habits of a beautiful young woman who is driven to repeat certain ritual acts of prostitution by the overpowering force of a shocking event in her earlier life. Gretta's fate is worked out in the northern town of Unionville, where she exists in a reasonably comfortable world, free of economic deprivation, social pressure and family influences. In this setting, she becomes a melodramatic case study in a very narrow field of determinism. By contrast, Claudelle is the daughter of a poor Piedmont sharecropper whose life exists back among the jimson weeds, tenant shacks and peckerwoods, amid characters with names like Lightsy Hushoure, Horace Haddbetter and Ching Guyler. Though the evocation of girls with no panties, clergymen with frigid wives, and fights in which people are impaled on car hood ornaments is perhaps formulaic, the southern rural setting adds both color and complication to Claudelle's situation. Once again, the people are more erratic and more interesting, given the larger scope for conflicting influences on their lives that is permitted by a context that allows poverty, class, history, custom and even climate to enrich their motivation, in addition to their own thwarted instincts and sudden impulses. Caldwell was intrigued in his fiction by the extent to which all seemingly civilized behavior was a mask for instincts, urges and thoughts that are conventionally controlled, and thus he continually experimented with degrees of impropriety in the actions and words of his characters. Such flagrant indecorousness was both shocking and apt in his poor white milieu, allowing him to explore thoroughly both what was correctable in human society and what was incorrigible in human nature. Outside this setting, his characters were not only less shocking but also less credible. They became special cases whose situations appeared more estranged from any common human condition than those of the poor whites, whose determinism was not limited to one particular sphere and who retained a certain mystery in their conduct. By contrast, characters from outside the multiple shaping forces of remote southern environments rarely faced the kinds of quandaries and contradictions in their nature and circumstances that might produce unexpected consequences. Their freedom from hunger, inertia, parochialism and exploitation ironically merely focused attention on their narrower compulsions rather than on any wider moral choices. Thus *Gretta* is grimly and monotonously fatalistic, as are the accounts of the other middle-class heroines of *The Last Night of Summer* (1963) and *Annette* (1973), while *Claudelle Inglish* retains Caldwell's earlier capacity to disturb, surprise and amuse, eliciting from C. Hugh Holman the judgment that it was "an almost flawless sexual comedy with the skill of story-telling and the exuberance of a Chaucerian fabliau" (96-97).

Unlike almost any other American writer, Caldwell was a simpler moralist and naturalist when he was *not* writing about the poor. Though he maintained a rigorous simplicity of language and form throughout his fictional career, in the novels of the first part of the cyclorama this simplicity existed in a complicated tension with the dense social context of the rural poor and with the fabulous nature of their inner lives. By the mid-1940s, Caldwell chose to leave these people in order to search for new subjects and topicality. Far from being an effort to exploit his previous material, it seemed an attempt to extend his enquiries into novel and

58   *Caldwell's Fiction*

more immediately relevant areas that ultimately proved less fruitful for his peculiar talents and vision. This effort had the ironic consequence, as Scott MacDonald has pointed out (xiv-xv), of damaging the reputation of his earlier works by provoking such critical dissatisfaction that his whole body of work came to be dismissed or ignored. Yet Caldwell produced, between 1932 and 1943, a body of fiction about poor people in America unrivaled in its capacity to see them simultaneously as logical symptoms of historical and economic determinism in a crisis-ridden society, and of human eccentricity, self-deception and foolishness in an absurd universe. It was a unique achievement and, if only inconsistently sustained in his later work, still more than enough to merit continued attention.

WORKS CITED

Arnold, Edwin T., ed. *Conversations with Erskine Caldwell*. Jackson: UP of Mississippi, 1988.
Bode, Carl. "Erskine Caldwell: A Note for the Negative." *College English* 17 (Mar. 1956): 357-59
Bourke-White, Margaret. *Portrait of Myself*. New York: Simon, 1963.
Broadwell, Elizabeth Pell, and Ronald Wesley Hoag. "The Art of Fiction LXII, Erskine Caldwell." *Paris Review* 86 (Winter 1982): 126-57.
Caldwell, Erskine. *Call It Experience: The Years of Learning How to Write*. New York: Duell, 1951.
_____. *Tragic Ground*. New York: Duell, 1944.
_____. *Writing in America*. New York: Phaedra, 1967.
"Caldwell's Collapse." *Time* 30 Aug. 1948: 82, 84.
Cowley, Malcolm. *And I Worked at the Writer's Trade*. New York: Viking, 1978.
Daniels, Jonathan. "American Lower Depths." *Saturday Review of Literature* 27 (14 Oct. 1944): 46.
Devlin, James E. *Erskine Caldwell*. Boston: Twayne, 1984.
Faulkner, William. *Faulkner at Nagano*. Tokyo: Kenkyusha, 1956.
Holman, C. Hugh. "Detached Laughter in the South." *Comic Relief: Humor in Contemporary American Literature*. Ed. Sarah Blacher Cohen. Urbana: U of Illinois P, 1978. 87-104.
Klevar, Harvey. "Some Things Holy in a Godforsaken Land." *Pembroke* 11 (1979): 65-76.
Korges, James. *Erskine Caldwell*. Minneapolis: U of Minnesota P, 1969.
MacDonald, Scott, ed. *Critical Essays on Erskine Caldwell*. Boston: Hall, 1981.
Smith, Harrison. "Well-Controlled Anger." *Saturday Review of Literature* 29 (18 May 1946): 8-9.
Tinkle, Lon. "Crumbled Georgia Crackers." *Saturday Review of Literature* 31 (28 Aug. 1948): 12-13.

Caldwell on Stage and Screen

WILLIAM L. HOWARD

Erskine Caldwell's works have often been held responsible for the simplistic and one-sided view of the South commonly found in our popular culture. Jack Kirby, for example, has argued in his discussion of the "media-made South" that Caldwell's emphasis on singular, extraordinary images failed to do justice to southern diversity and contributed strongly to the development of "pernicious abstractions" about the South. Before Caldwell can be indicted for misrepresenting his native region, however, it should be noted that large audiences knew him through sources other than his books. Several of his portraits of the South were adapted for other media. Not only were these adaptations often more popularly known and thus more influential than the originals, but each of them distorted to some extent Caldwell's artistic and social vision.

We should also note that Caldwell's voice, even when distorted or muffled through adaptations, still rang with truth to southerners of perception and integrity. The young Ralph Ellison, for example, found the southern portraits in the stage version of *Tobacco Road* not pernicious but liberating. He laughed so hard at the antics of the Lester family that he created a disturbance in the theatre (186). This "extravagance of laughter," as he termed it, was attributable to the shock of recognition he experienced when he saw dramatized on stage poor white characters from his southern past: "For all its intentional outrageousness, the comedy of *Tobacco Road* was deeply rooted in the crazy-quilt life I knew" (196).

The adaptations remain problematic, however, because they represent Caldwell as filtered through his adapters. As Ellison observed, the play of *Tobacco Road* operates on two levels. He could see the authenticity and comic brilliance of Caldwell's original conception beneath the "intentional outrageousness." Other viewers could not. John Donald Wade and the Agrarians may have been right to some extent when they predicted that Caldwell's work would only confirm northern prejudices.[1] But it is telling that the playwrights and filmmakers who adapted his works chose to make so many substantive alterations. They packaged their versions to correspond with popular audiences' preconceptions, sometimes deliberately to make the works more successful and sometimes because the adapters themselves could not understand the finer aspects of Caldwell's art and imposed their own aesthetic criteria and social orientations.

Careful analyses of the play and film versions of *Tobacco Road* and the later film adaptation of *God's Little Acre* reveal serious differences between these works and their sources, differences that alter to the detriment of its integrity Caldwell's message about southern life.

Before Jack Kirkland's 1933 adaptation of *Tobacco Road* for the stage, which became wildly popular and ran for seven and one-half years on Broadway, the American public was largely unaware of Erskine Caldwell. The novel had been published in 1932 when Caldwell was a young, relatively unknown author, and Scribner's, fearing the displeasure of its southern textbook clients, had not enthusiastically promoted it. Thus the American public's original impression of Jeeter Lester and his family derived almost exclusively from Kirkland's interpretation of the novel. Many who watched the play would never be exposed to the unadulterated version. Few cared about the differences between the two.[2]

Whereas Caldwell's style was hard-boiled and unflinching in its depiction of the unpleasant realities of a region in distress, Kirkland's was cliché-ridden, sentimental and sensational. He added, for example, an impending foreclosure which provided an inherently gripping dramatic situation, something arguably essential to the stage version. Such an addition was also in tune with the times and pandered to popular perceptions of rural reality: cruel economic forces threatened to separate a farmer from his beloved land. Kirkland's drama was meant to be popular Depression fare of the sort that would make *The Grapes of Wrath*, both the novel and the movie, popular at the end of the decade.

Additional dialogue also might be expected with the change to a genre that must communicate by voice and action rather than the written word. But the mystery surrounding a character's behavior in the novel, created by surrealistic silences that portray numbness, ignorance and suffering, was destroyed by Kirkland's substitution of obvious dialogue, obvious situations and poor-white clichés. The mysterious silence of Ellie May is replaced with "Aw, gee!" Ada, who spends most of the novel chewing on a snuff stick, generates laughs from the audience by kicking the napping Jeeter and saying, "Wake up, you old fool— Lov's coming." And Dude is made predictable by his obvious "bad boy" behavior: he threatens not to carry out his parents' wishes after they die, taunts his mother about Pearl's origins ("What was you doing, Ma, horsing around some man besides that old fool over there?"), encourages his father and mother's fighting ("Cuss the hell out of him, Ma"), throws the ball at his grandmother's head ("Look out of the way, old woman, or I'll knock your head off") and mentions that he would soon have to go to Fuller and steal himself a new baseball (Kirkland 634, 605, 603, 601). At the least, the amount and manner of these characters' talking contradict the brooding, usually silent grotesques of the novel and make stereotypes out of original conceptions.

Kirkland also encouraged character motivation that is at odds with Caldwell's naturalistic vision of reality. In the play, Ellie May falls in love with Lov Bensey rather than simply lusting after him, Ada is more concerned with a daughter who lives away from home than with her own hunger pains, Dude has a "fierce" ambition to own a car with a horn and Jeeter is obsessed with ownership of the land rather than simply with the land itself. In each case, an abstraction rather than a definite physical stimulus motivates the characters, a major revision of Caldwell's conception of poor-white life.

The impending foreclosure, although adding topical social context and suspense to the plot, also changed characters' motivations and revised Caldwell's sociological beliefs. The energy and desperation that become part of Jeeter's character when he sets out to save his farm do not conform with the procrastinating Jeeter of the book. Kirkland missed the essence of Jeeter's character when he showed him actively and tragically seeking to keep his land rather than passively unable to leave it. Caldwell maintained that the Lesters' habitual laziness and unwillingness to help themselves were the result of a lack of nutrition and proper medical care, just as the land's worthlessness was the result of improper farming techniques and years of abuse ("Writer First" 89). Thus, to make the breaking of the existential bond between the land and characters the crisis and the reason for the characters' actions defeats the purpose of Caldwell's story. The Lesters' problem is not the temporary one of losing the land but the continual one of making it feed them so they will not starve.

The climax of the play, although conceptually very ambitious, is no less foreign to Caldwell's conception of the Lesters. Ada is run over in a scene meant to show the heroic death of a strong woman and the tragic parting from her daughter. It is the stuff of classical mythology: a frantic Demeter trying desperately to pull her Persephone out of the clutches of Hades. The high tragedy with which this scene is invested, however, is not only a distortion of the novel's plot in which the grandmother is run over (a logical conclusion to the family's indifference to her) but is also inappropriate to the story of depraved Georgia sharecroppers. Caldwell's Ada shows no signs of altruism or energy. She is more interested in snuff than her daughter, just as Jeeter is more interested in eating turnips than sharing them with his family. The novel holds that unselfish motives are made impossible by the harsh facts of disease and hunger. It does not show a family that demonstrates signs of nobility in between moments of animalism.

With all the substantive differences—many of them directly contradicting his own artistic vision—why did Caldwell react so tolerantly to the play?[3] Why did he defend it from attacks as fiercely as he did his novel? There are several possible reasons. First, he must have felt that the attention given to the play was, at least partially, attention he deserved for having originated the story. He took the attacks on the play as personal attacks on himself (see "Of 'Tobacco Road'"). The situation came down to letting the critics go unanswered or vowing allegiance to the dramatization. A second reason for his taking sides with the play may be that he was still young and unsure of the distinctiveness of his own artistry: "I like the material Kirkland used, even if I would have used it in other ways. But maybe it will picture the book a little better to those who thought it was rotten" (9 Dec. 1933). A final reason for his tolerance of the play may have been his conception at that time of his role as an artist. If he seemed to dismiss form and aesthetics as unimportant, perhaps he preferred the role of artist/reformer, a role he was familiar with from his reading of *New Masses* and other leftist publications. If the purpose of the book was to call attention to the poverty that few Americans would acknowledge and if collaboration with a playwright, producer and actors called attention to it more effectively and on a grander scale than his novel did, then he would support the play. The story *had* to be told, however it was told and no matter what role he had in the telling.

Although Caldwell could accept the play made from his novel, he did, nevertheless, reject the subsequent film version. Two successful precedents had convinced Hollywood producer Darryl F. Zanuck to purchase the rights to the play. *Gone With the Wind*, released in 1939, had demonstrated that the public craved southern subject matter; *The Grapes of Wrath*, produced in 1940, had proven that audiences also liked depictions of Depression-era hard times. Zanuck's efforts to combine the two in a production of *Tobacco Road* can be detected in the film. Indeed, he retained both the director and screenwriter (John Ford and Nunnally Johnson) from *The Grapes of Wrath* in hopes of replicating the success of the earlier movie (Gomery 10). Because the film was an adaptation of the play rather than the novel, the tendency to violate Caldwell's artistic principles, to sacrifice the integrity of his story to audience expectations, was even more pronounced. The comic aspects of the Lesters' story was turned into farce, and the story was rendered hackneyed and sentimental.

The film, which premiered in 1941, begins with a narration by Jeeter Lester that attempts to fill in southern sociological and historical detail. Unlike the novel's hard, factual, social-scientific expositions by an objective narrator, the film sentimentally features Jeeter's telling the story of tobacco road country and the Lesters' place in it with melancholy snatches of "Dixie" playing in the background. The camera focuses on "a breath-taking mansion, the remnants of Tara Hall," complete with "eight majestic columns." Once part of a large estate, "it exists now only in its noble outlines" (Johnson).[4] The final words of the narration—"but all that they had and all that they were—that's all gone with the

William L. Howard
63

wind and the dust. And this, this is Tobacco Road today''—make the film sound like a sequel to *Gone With the Wind.*

The comedy of Kirkland's play was originally a "restrained" humor. As Caldwell remembered, "The first actor to take that part [of Jeeter Lester] was Henry Hull. Henry Hull was not a comic actor. He was a classic actor, and he did not play for laughs. He played the role precisely as the material dictated. And he succeeded to the extent that he was able to bring out any humor that existed in Jeeter without sacrificing any of the serious nature of the character. After Hull there were three or four other actors . . . and they played for laughs, made up lines. But the play was not a comedy" (Arnold 280). The film, however, made no pretense about its attitude toward the story. At the outset, Jeeter (Charlie Grapewin) is portrayed as a happy-go-lucky clown shouting "whoa!" to his battered Model T Ford pickup, which, according to one reviewer, "explodes as often as the trick clowns' car in the Ringling Bros. and Barnum & Bailey Circus" ("Tobacco" 88). Not seeming to care that three of the four tires are flat, Jeeter states ("cheerfully" according to the screenplay), "I can get home as long as I have one good one."

In the process of creating farce, the movie alters Jeeter's character significantly. Caldwell's Jeeter is not "cheerful" about adversity. He may not have concerned himself when things went wrong, but he was fully aware that things *were* wrong and hardly happy about the fact. Nor is the original Jeeter stupid. When he drives into the front yard of the Lester home in the film, we learn that he has been to Augusta for the fourth time with the same load of blackjack, still not having found a buyer. This hardheadedness directly contradicts the novel, in which, unable to find a buyer on his first and only trip to Augusta, Jeeter disgustedly (his manner itself suggesting the slim dignity the novel affords him) empties the car along the side of the road and tries to burn the wood. The fact that it refuses to stay on fire even after being doused in gasoline is humorous in the novel since he has been selling it for firewood, but the humor is not completely at Jeeter's expense. Moreover, when the film does try to portray Jeeter seriously, it can do so only by investing him with uncharacteristic sentimentality. In anticipation of his eviction, he looks around "the old place" trying to fix it in his mind: part of the *Gone With the Wind* syndrome. Caldwell's Jeeter is a character driven by biological forces, not nostalgia. His attachment to the land is sensual, not sentimental.

In Johnson's screenplay and in the film, characters are also distorted to make them more depraved than in the novel. In a scene from the screenplay, for example (absent from the film), Ada asks Jeeter for the snuff he was to buy her in town. He replies that he spent the dime on "what they call a PEEP-show," "the DURNDEST thing I ever did see!" In the film itself, Jeeter justifies the theft of the turnips from Lov (Ward Bond) with, "You cain't steal from your son-in-law 'cause he's—he's kinfolks.'' In the novel, Jeeter is ashamed of himself precisely because he stole from his own son-in-law.

Dude's ''bad boy'' irreverence is distorted as well. William Tracy sounds more like someone from the Bowery than a sixteen-year-old Georgian and, further, seems too old for the part. Changing Dude's age to twenty (sixteen in the novel) is a transparent cover. Talking from the side of his mouth as if in a James Cagney gangster movie, Dude taunts his father with the possibility that he will go to the Poor Farm and his mother with the assurance that she will not be buried in a new dress. He even pushes his father to the ground. Dude is not this obviously cruel in the novel.

Like Dude, Ellie May (Gene Tierney) is also altered, although the film actually restores some of the silent mystery that characterizes her in the novel.[5] The film dilutes her grotesque appearance and sexuality. She has no harelip. She slides across the yard to Lov demurely with her back to the camera; there is no sign of the missing panties that so fascinated Dude. The copulation in the front yard as the turnips are stolen is replaced with suggestive remarks such as ''Aint you gonna give me just a bite, Lov?'' and ''Just one little biddy bite, Lov?'' There is also a sexually provocative profile of her by a tree as Lov contemplates accepting her as a substitute wife. Much of the effect of these suggestions is lost, however, when Ellie May ''cleans herself up'' and, dressed in a white party dress with hat, runs off like a modest and beautiful girl, instead of the sexually overt grotesque she is in the novel, to keep house for Lov.

The dialogue of Lov Bensey rings true, although some of his motives are altered. When Ada asks, ''Is you treatin' [Pearl] right?'' Lov replies: ''What's that got to do with it? She's married to me, ain't she?'' And later when he returns to say Pearl has run away and Ada again is suspicious of his conduct, he defends himself: ''I wasn't doin' a thing in the world to that girl but tyin' her up with some rope.'' These lines are as humorous as in the novel. But his chief complaint in the novel and play—that Pearl will not sleep with him—is reduced to a complaint that she will not talk to him. Similarly, because Ellie May no longer has a physical impairment, Lov complains about her age, contending that at twenty-three, she is too old, and everyone would laugh at him for marrying such an old woman.

Caldwell's concept of Ada (Elizabeth Patterson) is significantly changed. She is used to support the pervasive religious theme in the film wherein hymn-singing and prayer come to substitute for sex. In one scene, Ada threatens Jeeter with God's curse if he does not confess to Bessie his sin of stealing Lov's turnips. This leads directly into a comic thunderstorm scene (not in the novel) in which Jeeter is convinced that God is displeased with him. In another scene, Bessie announces she is going to make Dude a preacher, and in the sentimental moment that follows (with ''Shall We Gather at the River'' in the background), Ada is plainly pleased by the prospect as she repeats to herself the news. In the scene in which Lov announces that Pearl has run away, Ada responds with a quiet "Praise the Lord," a response quite different from her response in the novel and play.

Rural religiosity, however, is most fully explored with Bessie (Marjorie Rambeau). The film makes much of her and Dude's trip to town to buy a car and get married, and her, Dude and Jeeter's trip to Augusta. Neither of these journeys, although part of the novel, was included in the play, perhaps because of staging difficulties or because they would have violated dramatic unity. Ford and Johnson, however, exploit the trips for comic effect and to further the religious theme. In the novel, Bessie prays in the showroom of the automobile dealership before the car she and Dude are about to buy. But the screenplay exaggerates this scene. Some people on the street notice the "service" going on inside the showroom and kneel down as well: in the scene directions, they do so "reluctantly but unwilling to go counter to a religious movement." Although the scene was not finally dramatized in this way, the absurd distortion of southern fervor survives as the film shows the salesmen and another customer unable to resist joining Bessie and Dude in the singing of "In the Sweet By and By."

The courthouse scene in which Bessie and Dude are denied a wedding license by a rude clerk further pursues the idea of southern religious expressiveness and conformity. In answer to the intractable bureaucrat, Bessie pulls out her pitch-pipe and starts singing "Bringing in the Sheaves." A woman clerk, according to the screenplay, "doubtfully" joins in followed by the Mayor, "an enthusiastic chorister," and the Coroner. The motives for their behavior? "Southern country people are all lovers of good loud hymn singing," according to the screenplay's directions. Soon everyone converges on the clerk's office singing, and he relents, gives them the license and starts singing himself. The scene is a long way from Caldwell's idea of southern fundamentalism.

Finally, the film makes social statements about sharecropping and the bank's role in foreclosures that are also very different from Caldwell's original. Following the play, the film includes the characters of Captain Tim (Dana Andrews) and Mr. Payne (Grant Mitchell). Two scenes with Mr. Payne seem to be correctives to Caldwell's left-leaning perspective. In the first, in Payne's bank office, Payne denies Jeeter a loan. The screenplay includes Payne's line (deleted from the film), "Oh, DARN this job, anyway!" Not the heartless banker of Depression legend, Payne is portrayed as really a decent person who, except for the limitations of his job, would help Jeeter. The same sentiment is demonstrated when Payne comes to the Lester farm to collect the rent just prior to Ada and Jeeter's eviction: "I hate this kind of thing about as much as anything in the world. . . . I haven't any choice." Jeeter reassures him that he is not to blame.

A similar political corrective is made near the end of the film. Jeeter and Ada, forsaken by their children and evicted from their land, are seen walking to the Poor Farm. Captain Tim picks them up and returns them home. Even though he cannot afford it, he has paid six months' rent to banker Payne so that Jeeter and Ada can remain on the land. "Dixie" is played quietly in the background throughout the scene, suggesting that good old southern traditions like peonage must be restored if people like the Lesters are to be happy. Tim also gives Jeeter ten dollars for seed and guano (for which Jeeter has sought in vain for seven years in the novel). Tenant farming is transformed into an American Dream story. Captain Tim: "I'm staking you for six months—to see if you can really grow yourself a crop this time. Think you can do it? . . . You can do it, Jeeter. You did it for my dad—you can do it for me." Jeeter replies, "The good Lord certainly looks out after the poor." This optimism was diametrically opposed to the attitude of the hard-nosed realist Erskine Caldwell.

Thus, Caldwell had many reasons for disliking the movie. To alienate him further, neither he nor Kirkland was consulted during production. During his employment in Hollywood as screenwriter in the thirties, he had learned to hate moguls and sympathize with the writers, directors and actors who were at their beck and call. It is not surprising, then, that in his reminiscences about the film, he expressed appreciation for the talents of John Ford and Nunnally Johnson and directed his resentment towards Zanuck, whom he called "the offending producer" ("Night" 110). Ford and Johnson, he would later note, had "some pretty good ideas . . . but Zanuck wouldn't let them do 'em" (Saha 20). Caldwell also resented Hollywood's power to influence his life. In a letter of 1934 he had complained bitterly about Hollywood efforts to "close the play" so that it could get James Barton, who was then playing Jeeter Lester on Broadway, to Hollywood: "Any studio that would try to close a play is a bunch of bastards, and those are the words I used," he wrote his friend Alfred Morang.

In his reminiscences, Caldwell called the film "an inadequate screen presentation of either the novel or the play" and "one of the most conspicuous failures in cinematic history" (*Call* 152; "Night" 110). He identified two reasons for the film's failure. First, it was produced during a time of "unrestrained censorship." He did not specify whether the censorship was of suggestive sexual behavior or of left-leaning political opinions. Judging from the film, he could have meant both. The second reason was "the film-maker's rejection of the reality of the story itself." Specifically, Caldwell cited the substitution of "an absurdly falsified happy ending" that effectively destroyed the central social idea in the novel ("Night" 110). His idea that the situation on tobacco road was so hopeless for both tenants and landlords that only government intervention could change it was subverted by having the landlord save his tenants to maintain their traditional family-like relationship.

It is, then, understandable that Caldwell supported the play but not the movie. If the play's reality was slightly askew, at least its unhappy ending was true to Caldwell's view of the tenants' existence. It did not try to dilute the intense economic or sexual reality of the people represented.

Anthony Mann's film adaptation of *God's Little Acre* in 1958 was considerably more faithful to the original novel than the *Tobacco Road* adaptations. Philip Yordan's screenplay used much of Caldwell's original language and plot, although it occasionally distorted the story to a watered-down version of the original.[6]

Like the novel, the film basically supports two themes—love and labor. Despite all its sexuality, there is no conventional love story in Caldwell's novel, perhaps no romantic love between man and woman at all. But such a theme is added to the film to soften the sheer, animalistic sexual drives that attracted some eight million readers to the book. For example, Darling Jill (Fay Spain) and the albino (Michael Landon), rather than copulating under the nearest tree, float romantically on a rowboat out into a pond. Similarly, Will Thompson (Aldo Ray) and Griselda (Tina Louise), rather than being attracted solely on an animalistic level, have a nostalgic base to their relationship. Supposedly, they have had a prior relationship when they both worked in a mill together; Will bought her her first pair of high heels which she wore proudly in the mill; they were going to get married, but Griselda wanted to live in the country, and he would not leave the milltown. These details certainly alter the perception of a relationship that, in the novel, has only recently begun when Will tears Griselda's clothes off in front of his own wife.

The labor theme in the film, despite the realistic scenes that attend it, is also watered down. The camera shots of the men standing before the darkened mill in a silently seething vigil, Will's shaking of the mill fence that symbolizes the forces keeping him from doing his life's work, the cheering crowd when the lights go on in the mill, the somberness of the crowd as they carry Will's body from the mill in a death march: all are impressively filmed and would have gratified leftist critics of the novel who complained of a lack of social realism. But there are also significant emendations to the ideological orientation of the novel, perhaps because 1958 was not long after the McCarthy era and there was a fear of seeming to take the Communist line. The most notable of these comes with Will's death. Instead of being killed by strikebreakers, he is shot by a doddering old night watchman who, waving his gun scoldingly, shoots him accidentally. This certainly dilutes the political impact of the story, almost as completely as the happy ending in *Tobacco Road* diluted Caldwell's social statement about the impoverished inhabitants of tobacco road.

Ty Ty Walden (Robert Ryan), like Jeeter before him, is sentimentalized and revised for the film audience. He discusses his gold lust in terms of his grandfather's having buried the gold 100 years before, so that digging for it seems a family custom. Although the novel does mention the grandfather's burying the gold, the obsession is clearly Ty Ty's personal compulsion, not an act of familial reverence. The film also blunts Caldwell's ironic portrayal of Ty Ty as a type of southern transcendentalist living on his own Walden Pond. The whole point of the novel's portrait of Ty Ty is that while he mouths his love for land and family, his actions are contrary and cause the very destruction he wished to avoid. Ty Ty's son Jim Leslie is murdered by his brother Buck with a shotgun when Jim Leslie tries to take Griselda away. Buck then goes off to commit suicide with the same gun, and Ty Ty is left surveying a wasteland. As Caldwell wrote, "He wished then that he had the strength to spread out his arms and smooth the land as far as he could see, leveling the ground by filling the holes with the mounds of earth. He realized how impotent he was by his knowledge that he would never be able to do that" (*God's Little Acre* 157). When he returns to his digging, he is, at least symbolically, digging a grave for his sons and perhaps for himself as well.

The ending of the film, however, demonstrates Hollywood's smoothing of the rough edges of Caldwell's reality. There is no murder on Ty Ty's land. Ty Ty throws himself on Jim Leslie just as Buck is about to pinion him with a pitchfork. No blood is spilled on God's little acre. Ty Ty rises in righteous indignation and orders Jim Leslie off his land forever. Recognizing his own culpability, Ty Ty vows "never to dig another hole again." In the next scene, the holes are covered over and crops are being planted. The newly elected sheriff, Pluto Swint (Buddy Hackett), drives up with siren blowing to a faithfully waiting Darling Jill. Griselda, having gotten over Will's death, brings refreshments to her husband, the hard-plowing and contented Buck (Jack Lord) whose only desire is "to be waited on by a beautiful woman." The ending is saved from total sentimentality only by a comic reassertion of Ty Ty's irredeemable and irrepressible nature. He finds a broken shovel in the ground while plowing which he gathers is the shovel of his grandfather. Assuming that this discovery could only signify gold buried nearby, he again begins digging. The camera returns to the opening shot of the movie—the Walden pond—but this time the cross marking God's little acre leans in the water, a clever device that symbolizes Ty Ty's cockeyed and amusing personality.

Caldwell's comments on the movie in a 1958 interview with Carvel Collins reveal that he was satisfied with Mann and Yordan's adaptation. He believed it showed "the essence and the atmosphere of the novel." It gave him pleasure because it "enhanced the book in some way" "like an illustrated edition" (22, 24). In another interview of the same year, he remarked, "The film is quite like the book . . . in that it opens where the book begins and closes where the book ends" ("Talk"). He seemed unaware that the film, like the hated movie version of *Tobacco Road*, had an optimistic conclusion at odds with the novel.

Erskine Caldwell with Robert Ryan, who starred as Ty Ty Walden in Anthony Mann's film version of *God's Little Acre* (1958).

As long as the film did not contradict sociological reality, it seems Caldwell could live with it.[7] Whereas the *Tobacco Road* film as a whole failed to capture the reality of the Lesters in a serious way (the ending epitomizing its overall misconception of Caldwell's intentions), *God's Little Acre* in many respects did justice to the book, its ending clearly supporting tendencies established in the novel even though it contradicted the novel's tragic vision of the Walden family's future. While the novel's ending asserts a tragic and chaotic view of mankind, the end of the film reasserts the more comic and optimistic view established earlier.

Unlike the adapters of his work, Caldwell wrote about the South without exploiting his subject matter. While northern audiences often regarded the adaptations as farce and southern critics cringed that the South should be held up to ridicule, Caldwell neither ridiculed nor cringed. In his novels, as well as in his remarks on them, he consistently expressed respect and often affection for his characters, despite their vices and ignorance. His first wife Helen gave a clue to his intentions in a 1935 interview in which she was asked about the *Tobacco Road* play: "I believe Southern people will understand it," she said, "and realize that Erskine wrote out of compassion and understanding and brotherliness about a man whose fine qualities survive even the lowest, bitterest deprivations."

The evidence of artistry in Caldwell's novels is never more apparent than when contrasted to the adaptations made of his works. Caldwell's brilliant private vision (private in spite of his awareness of social causes and social rhetoric) is often made banal in the adaptations, warped to the public's expectations and to the adapters' limited understanding of his ultimate intentions. If nothing else, the adaptations show by contrast the complexity and integrity of Caldwell's work and make clear the originality of Caldwell's vision and style.

NOTES

[1]Wade argued that Caldwell's stories "deal... with just the sort of people that sophisticated New Yorkers and would-be New Yorkers—the major part of the book-buying population of America—can at once most envy and marvel over and deplore, with the sort of people best calculated to satisfy at once the current vogue for primitivism and the constant vogue of metropolitan complacency" (453).

[2]Even today, critics confuse them. Douglas Gomery's 1978 study of the novel, play and film, for example, shows a lack of familiarity with the novel. Gomery assumes that the plot, like the plots of the play and film, hinges on the impending loss of the land: "Caldwell devotes much space to recreating Jeeter's fearful thoughts on the matter." He also states that Grandmother Lester, "a victim of technology," is run over by her own car (11). There is also evidence that Caldwell himself came to recall the play more readily than the novel, perhaps even fusing the two in his mind ("Writer First" 93; "Night" 102-04).

³Right after the premier, he told I. L. Saloman that the dramatization "probably wouldn't be much different than it is now" even if he had had more to do with its writing. "I thought it best to let Kirkland do it in his own way; and personally I think he did well considering the fact that it was novel-material, and not play-material, to begin with" (16 Dec. 1933). In his later years, he spoke fondly of the play, recalling that he had seen it "no less than two dozen times." He was satisfied that Kirkland was "a Southerner by birth, like myself" and "was familiar with both the era and locale of the novel" ("Night" 102).

⁴All references to the film are to *Tobacco Road*, directed by John Ford, Twentieth Century Fox, 1941. References to Nunnally Johnson's unpublished screenplay "Tobacco Road" are distinct from references to the film because the two versions often differ. Johnson's name or the term *screenplay* refers to material exclusively from the screenplay; otherwise, references are to the film itself.

⁵The restoration of her silences may have been Ford's idea, for Johnson's screenplay gives her dialogue that has the same effect as her dialogue in the play. It destroys her mystery and makes her new alliance with Lov at the end of the screenplay a sentimental love story: "Ma, I'm plumb crazy for him!"

⁶Caldwell was a partner in the production of this film. He joined with Philip Yordan (screenwriter), Anthony Mann (director) and Sidney Harmon (producer) to form an independent film company called Security Pictures. Each member contributed his own skill to the *God's Little Acre* project, although it is not clear how much work Caldwell did on the screenplay (see below). United Artists underwrote the effort with a one million dollar contribution.

⁷The film was not always so closely related to the novel. In fact, a first draft of the *God's Little Acre* screenplay resembles the *Tobacco Road* screenplay in its numerous, needless distortions of the novel. It opens with Ty Ty seeking a loan in a bank and ends with Buck grinning wistfully as Griselda and Jim Leslie leave the Walden place to get married (in this version, Buck and Griselda are dating but not married). Characters are altered considerably. Ty Ty feels like "licking the floor till my tongue would've been as full of splinters as an old shingle roof." Jim Leslie, a used-car salesman, refers to Ty Ty as "Papa," attempts to negotiate an end to the mill strike, decides not to marry a rich widow and wins Griselda's hand. The rather sexless Will is unheroically shot in the foot after turning the power on. In short, Ty Ty is mealy-mouthed, Jim Leslie incorrupt, Will less potent, Buck less savage and sexual affairs nonadulterous.

Found in the Dartmouth Caldwell collection, this typescript was contributed by Caldwell to a 1969 public benefit auction. In a letter to Matthew J. Bruccoli, Caldwell calls it "the first draft (corrected) of the screenplay treatment done in 1955 for the film 'God's Little Acre.'" Although the letter does not actually say that the work is Caldwell's own, the fact that it is typed on his beloved yellow paper suggests that it is. If so, Caldwell would seem to have had as much trouble recapturing his vision of the 1930s as his adapters did, or else he was severely hampered by censorship.

WORKS CITED

Arnold, Edwin T. "Interview with Erskine Caldwell." *Conversations with Erskine Caldwell.* Jackson: UP of Mississippi, 1988. 265-96.

Caldwell, Erskine. *Call It Experience.* New York: Duell, 1951.

_____. *God's Little Acre.* 1933. New York: Signet, 1971.

_____. Interview. "Erskine Caldwell at Work." *Atlantic Monthly.* With Carvel Collins. July 1958: 21-27. (Rpt. in Arnold 38-51.)

_____. Interview. "Talk with the Writer." *Newsweek* 2 June 1958: 90.

_____. Interview. "A Writer First: An Interview with Erskine Caldwell." With Ronald Wesley Hoag and Elizabeth Pell Broadwell. *Georgia Review* 36 (1982): 83-101. (Rpt. in Arnold 160-78.)

_____. Letter to Matthew J. Bruccoli. 12 Sept. 1969. Dartmouth Collection.

_____. Letter to Alfred Morang. 26 July 1934. Sutton Collection.

_____. Letter to I. L. Saloman. 9 Dec. 1933; 16 Dec. 1933. Sutton Collection.

_____. "A Night in November/ Beverly Hills, California." *Georgia Review* 36 (1982): 102-11.

_____. "Of 'Tobacco Road.'" *New York Times* 10 May 1936: 1-2X.

Caldwell, Helen. Interview. With Frank Daniel. Sutton Collection. (Published in the *Atlanta Journal*, 1935.)

Dartmouth College Caldwell Collection. Includes typescripts of most of the published novels, a *God's Little Acre* screenplay, personal letters and business papers. Hanover, NH.

Ellison, Ralph. "An Extravagance of Laughter." *Going to the Territory.* New York: Random, 1986. 145-97.

God's Little Acre. Dir. Anthony Mann. With Robert Ryan, Aldo Ray and Tina Louise. Security Pictures, 1958.

Gomery, Douglas. "Three Roads Taken: The Novel, the Play, and the Film." *The Modern American Novel and the Movies.* Ed. Gerald Peary and Roger Shatzkin. New York: Ungar, 1978. 9-18.

Johnson, Nunnally. "Tobacco Road." Unpublished screenplay. 25 Nov. 1940. Rare Book Room, U of Illinois Library.

Kirby, Jack. *Media-Made Dixie: The South in the American Imagination.* Baton Rouge: Louisiana State UP, 1978.

_____. "The South as a Pernicious Abstraction." *Perspectives on the American South: An Annual Review of Society, Politics and Culture.* Ed. Merle Black and John Shelton Reed. Vol. 2. New York: Gordon, 1984. 167-79.

Kirkland, Jack. *Tobacco Road.* 1933. *20 Best Plays of the Modern American Theatre.* Ed. John Gassner. New York: Crown, 1949. 599-642.

Saha, Mark. "Two Encounters." Unpublished essay. Sutton Collection.

Sutton, William A. Sutton collection. Rare Book Room, U of Illinois Library. Includes unpublished biography of Erskine Caldwell, copies of manuscripts, Caldwell correspondence, transcriptions of Scribner's correspondence (originals at Princeton U Library), Frank Daniel's interview with Helen Caldwell and Mark Saha's unpublished essay "Two Encounters."

Tobacco Road. Dir. John Ford. With Charlie Grapewin. Twentieth Century Fox, 1941.

"Tobacco Road." Rev. of *Tobacco Road* (movie). *Time* 37 (10 Mar. 1941): 88-89.

Wade, John Donald. "Sweet Are the Uses of Degeneracy." *Southern Review* 1 (1935-36): 449-66.

Canonize Caldwell's *Georgia Boy*:
A Case for Resurrection

RONALD WESLEY HOAG

Morris Stroup is no saint, but he deserves to be saved. Also worthy of salvation are his wife, Martha; his son, William; his yardboy, Handsome Brown; his jailbird brother, Ned; and an assortment of preachers, grass widows, gypsy queens, town marshals, necktie salesladies, ridgepole goats, shirt-tail woodpeckers, enticed calves and entrapped dogs, a triumphant fighting cock and a heartbreaking chicken pot pie. If it were up to me, I would elect them all, the whole damned circus and menagerie. Lamentable indeed is the moribund state of so much life, the more so in an age of canon revision. Unsustained by the adrenaline of his early public sensation, the literary vitality of Erskine Caldwell now depends on just two works, *Tobacco Road* (1932) and *God's Little Acre* (1933), the only major titles among his almost sixty books available in the paperback format necessary for classroom study and the limited immortality that it confers. To that short list I would add, at a minimum, the story cycle *Georgia Boy* (1943), currently out of print. The case for this recommendation may be expressed syllogistically. First, in order best to judge a writer's achievement, we must include a judgment of his work at its finest. Second, both Caldwell and a quorum of commentators have cited his stories as his best work and the *Georgia Boy* collection as the apex of his achievement in the form. Therefore, for our own enrichment and in fairness to Caldwell, we need to resurrect *Georgia Boy* for the extended reconsideration it deserves.

Although some critics have dismissed *Georgia Boy* as flawed and trivial, the book's structural integrity and thematic depth should rank it with another major American story cycle, Sherwood Anderson's *Winesburg, Ohio*. Far from being a loosely articulated constellation of simple stories, *Georgia Boy* is unified by contrapuntal characterization and a related animal motif, by dialogue refrains, by a complexly comic tone calling for varied reader responses, and by the twofold theme of coming of age in the South and the South's coming of age—a theme developed through a deceptively naive narrative perspective that requires our careful examination of the title itself. After briefly describing the book and its critical reception to date, I will offer my analytical defense—intended to be suggestive rather than exhaustive—of this largely overlooked and disregarded work.

73

Georgia Boy is the fictional account of fourteen episodes in the quirky life of the Stroup family of rural, turn-of-the-century Georgia. The principal figure in the book is Morris, a quixotic free spirit with a penchant for vagabonding, philandering and hopelessly impractical scheming. Engagingly incorrigible, he is to an extent suppressible by Martha, the locus of stability in *Georgia Boy*, whose mission is to keep home and household together by pulling Morris back whenever he goes too far. While good, Martha is not too good to be likable. For example, when Morris lures home Pretty Sooky, an irresistible calf belonging to a neighbor, Martha's righteous censure soon turns to complicity. This aberration humanizes her *character*, in two senses of the word. That both elder Stroups are sympathetically portrayed strengthens the book by complicating its world view.

The medium of sympathy in *Georgia Boy* is the narrator, William Stroup. He is a late preadolescent who appreciates his mother's sense and decency although he is drawn to the romantic model of his father. Observant and impressionable, he provides a superficially simple narrative viewpoint that is an artistic success for reasons to be discussed. The remaining member of the Stroup entourage is the family's black retainer, Handsome Brown. About the same age as his friend William, Handsome is akin to Martha in his emerging sensibleness and propriety; indeed, when she is not present to admonish Morris personally, Handsome often functions as her surrogate cautionary voice. Treated by Morris variously as a second son, slave, companion and scapegoat, Handsome is leery of his employer's thoughtless abuse even as he obviously enjoys the intermittent status of fishing buddy and quasi member of the family. Handsome's unstable position complicates and lends interest to the essentially similar story lines, wherein Morris ingeniously lands in trouble either to get out of it or meet his comeuppance.

Despite the dearth of criticism on Caldwell in general and his stories in particular, *Georgia Boy* has accrued some noteworthy favorable attention, not the least of which is Caldwell's own often-expressed opinion. Throughout his long career, Erskine Caldwell repeatedly cited *Georgia Boy* as his greatest achievement in the short-story form; and on those occasions when he was pressed to choose a single favorite from his many books, he named *Georgia Boy* most often. In 1961 he termed it "the most complete book I have ever written," adding that "it has everything, sociology, economics." He concluded, "I believe it will hold up longer than any other book I have written. . . . It goes into people more" (Guccione 55). In the first extended study of Caldwell, James Korges called the "neglected" *Georgia Boy* "one of the finest novels of boyhood in American literature" (5), lauding its blend of pathos and humor along with a "flawless handling of the point of view" (39). And in his final essay on Caldwell, Malcolm Cowley praised *Georgia Boy* as the author's last significant book. "I feel angry with recent critics," he declared, for "neglecting" this and other important

Caldwell works ("Caldwell's Magic" 6-7). [1] Henry Seidel Canby also was impressed, declaring that "it would be hard to find much more amusing reading" than the "perfectly delightful stories in *Georgia Boy*" (217-18).

Not all responses have been favorable, however, and at least two commentators have found *Georgia Boy* seriously flawed. In an essay published just three years after the book itself, W. M. Frohock termed the collection funny but "facile" (203). "There is no point in claiming that it is a great or even a significant book," he said. Rather, *Georgia Boy* is simply "something like what Mark Twain might have done had he come from Georgia and found himself in a playful mood" (202). More recently (1984) and more damagingly (because it is the only comprehensive, book-length study of Caldwell), James E. Devlin's *Erskine Caldwell* dismisses *Georgia Boy* as too inconsequential to be really good. Says Devlin: "The stories . . . for the most part, are extraordinarily slight. That is not to say that familiar topics such as the sex drive and racial injustice are altogether ignored. They are not; but they are touched on in such a manner as to escape the serious attention they command in more substantial works" (130). Devlin places the blame for the alleged slightness on the narrator, William. Unlike Huck Finn, who responds sensitively to the suffering and confusion he encounters, William, says Devlin, "is more like a camera who [sic] accords equal importance to everything in range." Censuring this perceived indifference, Devlin contends that "the book's objectivity, in its unfavorable sense, becomes overwhelming" (131). Curiously, Devlin here records as a fault what Malcolm Cowley, in a predecessor to his already-cited essay, applauded as a virtue. In Caldwell's writing, said Cowley, too often "the intrusion of moral feeling spoils the comedy, making you hesitate to laugh." He added, however, that although this problem is present in all the novels, the stories generally escaped the moralist's heavy hand. "The poet alone, with his wild humor, is responsible for . . . 'The Night My Old Man Came Home'" ("Two Caldwells" 200). This example of an unspoiled story is a representative selection from *Georgia Boy*. I will demonstrate that there is more of what Caldwell termed sociology and economics in the book than either Cowley or Devlin allows, although, as the former rightly affirmed, the essential humor does escape uncompromised, if not unqualified.

One excellent reason for bringing back *Georgia Boy* is its intriguing form. Structurally, the book is a bona fide story cycle akin to Sherwood Anderson's *Winesburg, Ohio*, among the few writers and titles that Caldwell admitted to admiring. Indeed, Malcolm Cowley went so far as to suggest that "most of his [Caldwell's] early stories could not have been written without the encouragement offered by *Winesburg, Ohio*, which served as a beacon light to many new talents of that age" ("Georgia Boy" 324). Even the evolution of the two books ran a parallel course. Like *Winesburg, Ohio*, *Georgia Boy* had its beginnings in independently conceived and separately published stories, stories nonetheless linked by shared settings, characters and a recurrent narrator. For both writers the emerging notion of a story cycle—that is, a work functioning not just as a collection of discrete stories but as a novel-like, articulated whole—impelled them to write additional episodes to round out their books and pull them together.

In Caldwell's case, eight of the fourteen stories in *Georgia Boy* were published there for the first time.[2] This simultaneous appearance of more than half of the book's contents is a corrective to the misconception, partially fostered by Caldwell himself, that *Georgia Boy* is not an integrated whole. His various statements that the stories were written independently over a number of years and that, as he told an interviewer in 1983, "I had no idea I would write enough to make a book" (Bonetti 248) are true only of the earlier, separately published stories and most probably not for all of them, especially those several published in the year or two immediately preceding the book itself. His most accurate explanation of the development of *Georgia Boy* is apparently one of his last, a 1986 statement that "I had started writing these episodes . . . and I just continued because I had the whole book in mind and wanted to do a whole, book-length series" (Arnold 288).[3] Clearly, Caldwell recognized and approved of the hybrid shape of his book. He said in 1958, "It could be that it is the ideal form as far as I am concerned: it can be divided into parts and yet the whole put together is a novel" (Collins 45). *Georgia Boy* is emphatically in the great tradition of English language story cycles, the distinguished lineage of which is traceable all the way back to the *Canterbury Tales* of Chaucer. The Stroup family stories must therefore be considered in a context that dictates the greater worth of the whole compared to the sum of the separate parts.

Like the almost certain model of *Winesburg, Ohio*, two of Caldwell's own earlier works suggest our consideration of *Georgia Boy* as a meaningfully and deliberately unified book. Although all three sections of his long prose-poem *The Sacrilege of Alan Kent* (1936) appeared initially as independent publications, their development was a continuous evolution, their final merger a natural combination. *The Sacrilege of Alan Kent* manifestly functions as a whole. Even more to the point, Caldwell's story collection *Jackpot*, published in 1940, combined into a single story three pieces, published separately elsewhere, that would later appear as chapters in *Georgia Boy*. "My Old Man" includes "The Night My Old Man Came Home," "Handsome Brown and the Aggravating Goats" and "My Old Man Hasn't Been the Same Since." In his brief *Jackpot* preface to "My Old Man," Caldwell said: "I read the first part of this story and immediately wrote the second. Afterwards I went back and read the first part for the second time, and straightway wrote the third part" (193). These successful combinative experiments in his own publishing history show that Caldwell was well prepared to execute a longer story cycle, especially one based on the Stroups.

The essential unity of *Georgia Boy* is best demonstrated by the book itself. One of the principal structuring devices here is Caldwell's deft employment of contrapuntal characterization. Morris and Martha are portrayed as polar opposites with more or less alternating moments of control over one another. Meanwhile, Handsome Brown—sometimes by inclination and sometimes by victimization— moves from one magnetic field to the other. Taking in all of this activity and making his report to the reader is the ever-watchful narrator, William. In a 1980 interview Caldwell alluded to this volatile characterization: "Martha was more dominant than Morris, certainly, but he was more animated than she was. In fact, I don't think there would have been any story at all without his animation. Just her role alone was not strong enough. When you write a story, you have to have a contrast between light and dark, high and low" (Broadwell and Hoag, "Southern Realism" 201). The seesawing of the Morris-Martha struggle moves the book along, making the conclusions of separate stories doubly significant because they also mark shifts in the relative ascendancy of the major characters. Against this lively context of dynamic equilibrium, the final stasis of the last chapter becomes especially noteworthy. When Martha kills the feisty rooster College Boy in "My Old Man Hasn't Been the Same Since," she symbolically cuts off her wayward husband's "cock." The story's last-word location in the book and the suggestion of final resolution in its title seemingly tilt the balance once and for all in favor of Martha and domestic virtue, leaving the reader to place that new reign of tranquility on the continuum of gain and loss.

As anyone who has read *Tobacco Road* knows, Erskine Caldwell was adept at exploiting similarities between people and animals for a variety of literary purposes. Snout-nosed Sister Bessie and fanny-dragging Ellie May make that book, in certain parts, something like a comic, naturalistic beast fable. In *Georgia Boy*, too, animal imagery functions as a major motif, employed here as an adjunct to structure, characterization and theme. Although the animals and humans in *Georgia Boy* are separate entities, the former help to catalyze and define the latter: characters are revealed by the animals they react against, respond to or imitate.

Martha particularly objects to roof-climbing goats, while Morris cannot abide impertinent woodpeckers. Handsome Brown reluctantly has his hands full with both species. The controversies surrounding these two episodes establish for the reader the pecking order in the Stroup household. Yet all is not turmoil here, for the darling calf Pretty Sooky proves too tempting for wife and husband alike. Martha's soft spot for this bovine "stray" and her willingness to look the other way in a potential moral crisis help the reader understand both her attraction to and tolerance for the philandering Morris. Structurally, "My Old Man and Pretty

Sooky'' sets up two other episodes involving Morris's penchant for collecting strays—"My Old Man's Political Appointment," with its similarly baited stray dogs, and "The Night My Old Man Came Home," with its pretty young stray of another kind. In the latter story, a whimsically inebriated Morris brings home a diminutive girlfriend who, he somehow thinks, will be accepted by Martha in the manner of Pretty Sooky. When Martha instead ends up in a hair-pulling brawl with the girl, Morris bemusedly picks apart the family furniture for drunken recreation. This humorously drawn domestic disturbance sets up, in turn, the bittersweet irony of the last animal story in *Georgia Boy*, the book's final chapter in which the bantam College Boy, spiritual double to Morris, loses his life to the fed-up Martha. Thus, the patterned and, to a degree, incremental use of the animal motif both moves the story cycle along and provides its closure.

An aspect of style in *Georgia Boy* that has received mention, but not attention, is the rhetorical use of repetition.[4] Specifically, dialogue refrains serve to link episodes and establish character. When Martha is about to reprimand Morris, she customarily first orders William to "go in the house right this instant and shut the doors and pull down all the window shades" (141). These directives and their occasions help to identify all three Stroups: she is the scolding parent to her childish husband and the sheltering parent to her child son. Her latter function also elucidates William's disinclination to judge the events he observes. Clearly, he has been habituated not to concern himself with the affairs of adults. For a child of contentious parents, there is no doubt a measure of comfort in such disengagement.

The reader comes to anticipate, in addition, characteristic utterances by both Morris and Handsome Brown. Typical of Morris are his incantations at the commencement of his schemes, for example: "We'll have more money than we'll know what to do with. . . . It's a shame I didn't know about this way of making money before, because it's the easiest way I ever heard of" (9). Typical also are his repeated stiflings of Handsome: "Shut up, Handsome. . . . Mind your own business" (166). Handsome, however, is delineated by his vain attempts to avoid entanglement in Morris's imbroglios and by his equally futile efforts to explain his involvement to Martha. "Sometimes I get a little mixed up when I try to tell the truth in both directions at the same time," he tells her in one such dilemma (140). His comment accurately portrays his pawnlike position. Yet perhaps even more powerless than Handsome is the narrator of *Georgia Boy* himself. William's first words to his parents in the opening episode of the book establish his disenfranchised status as a little boy: "Can't I, Ma? Can't I go see what it was?" (3). "I'll help, Pa. . . . Let me help, Pa" (4). In these as in similar instances, his beseechings are to no avail.

Tone, too, is a unifying element in *Georgia Boy* as well as a vehicle for advancing theme. Although the tone of all the stories might broadly be labeled as comic, the comedy ranges from farce ("My Old Man's Political Appointment") to fabliau ("My Old Man and the Gypsy Queen") to social satire ("The Time Handsome Brown Ran Away") to tall tale ("Handsome Brown and the Aggravating Goats") to domestic comedy of both a genial and melancholy sort ("My Old Man and Pretty Sooky" and "My Old Man Hasn't Been the Same Since," respectively). As often as not, a story calls for more than one reader response by employing different kinds of humor for different purposes. For example, the three episodes in which Handsome Brown is indirectly or directly abused by Morris ("Handsome Brown and the Aggravating Goats," "Handsome Brown and the Shirt-tail Woodpeckers" and "The Time Handsome Brown Ran Away") may be laughed at, if taken with a grain of salt as tall-tale exaggerations. They should, however, also be read—especially the last one—as social satires in which the real butt of the joke is not Handsome but rather the caste system that fosters such misuse. Because James Devlin neglects the important role of satire in these stories, he mistakes black humor for humor at the expense of blacks (131-32).

Similarly complex in their seriocomic tone are the stories in which Morris strives to rise in the world by an assortment of cockeyed get-rich-quick schemes. The episodes involving the baling of paper, the collecting of scrap iron and the rounding up of baited dogs are supposed to be antically funny, of course. There is poignancy here as well, however, for these stories present a man's continuously frustrated, and therefore pathetic, efforts to grow wealthy in a land of stunted opportunity. Witness, also, the condition of Handsome Brown as a post-emancipation economic slave. That the American Dream has not found realization in this Georgia hinterland community can make both man and boy do some funny things. To the reader falls the responsibility of deciding when laughter is appropriate.

An important structural link in *Georgia Boy* is the book's overarching theme, the coming of age of southerners and the South. One aspect of this comprehensive theme is what Leo Marx referred to as the "machine in the garden." The earlier example of Sister Bessie's automobile in *Tobacco Road* demonstrates that Caldwell was clearly aware of the impact of the machine age on the countryside and on country folk. Several stories in *Georgia Boy* involve this collision. The device that gives "My Old Man's Baling Machine" its title swallows up even Martha's collection of old "love and courtship letters" (14) as Morris fervently pursues his latest version of better living through technology. Similarly, in "The Time Ma Spent the Day at Aunt Bessie's," his harvesting of scrap iron for industry scavenges all but the shoes off the village horses' hooves. And in "Uncle Ned's Short Stay," the Coast Line freight train carries convict Ned and trouble to Martha's doorstep. Although *Georgia Boy* is essentially a rural nostalgia piece, the pastoral it presents is not simple and sentimental, but irretrievably compromised.

As to what the character of the new South will be when maturity finally arrives, Caldwell here offers two contending possibilities in the models of Morris and Martha, with a strong suggestion that the future will side with the latter. Neither a lazy William Byrd "lubberlander" nor an Al Capp Dogpatch derelict, Morris Stroup is, instead, a spiritual son of Simon Suggs, the Johnson Jones Hooper character who proclaims, "It is good to be shifty in a new country" (207). Shifty, not shiftless, describes Morris. With a little better luck he could pass for a Snopes, that clan of once-poor whites whose more illustrious members recognized that the turn from agrarianism to mercantilism could be turned to their advantage. Morris's back may flare up whenever Martha wants some household labor performed, but he is tireless in the service of his own designs. His willingness to bale up even his love letters to his wife, cheerfully exchanging these emblems of the family bond for a modest financial gain, indicates one of the forces pulling at the thread of southern life. That this homely fabric will hold, however, is implied by Martha's final domination over Morris at the end of the book. "My Old Man Hasn't Been the Same Since" is Erskine Caldwell's rendition of Stephen Crane's "The Bride Comes to Yellow Sky" and Mary Wilkins Freeman's "The Revolt of Mother." What those stories said about the Far West and New England, Caldwell's said for the Old South—that is, when the dust of change settles, civilization and domesticity will prevail over the gambles of boyish men who refuse to grow up. In a country no longer new, shiftiness has lost its sanction.

Another manifestation of coming of age in *Georgia Boy* is what critics have termed, with reference to Mark Twain and Sherwood Anderson, the "revolt from the village." Whether by influence or confluence, Caldwell's book exhibits in muted form this same revolt from provinciality. There is, however, a significant difference. The actual flight of Huck Finn and George Willard is only latently present in *Georgia Boy*, nascent in the not yet fully fledged William Stroup. When the social and economic injustices that William records lead, with his own maturing, to ethical rejection, presumably then will revulsion find expression in revolt. Certainly, such revolt lies at the heart of many other Caldwell works, both fiction and nonfiction.

Bridging all fourteen stories in his role of narrator, William Stroup is both observer of and player in the drama of coming of age. In a 1982 interview, Caldwell indicated that William is a boy of "ten or twelve years old" (Kehl 239).[5] This age is crucial to our understanding of the narrator and his narration. As a preadolescent, William has not yet reached the stage of second-guessing the adult world. Instead, he is at an age when bonding to and imitating both his parents largely prohibit rebellion. Otherwise objective in his narration, he does, however, become emotionally engaged in two of the last three stories, wherein he is forced to respond to severely divisive family crises. In the first instance, that response is passive and private. In the second, though, his assertive judgment upon a parental act marks his incipient emergence from boyhood, the significant note oñ which *Georgia Boy* ends.

In the twelfth episode, "The Night My Old Man Came Home," even as Martha battles the girlfriend and besotted Morris wrecks the furniture, William nonetheless gives thanks for his footloose father's presence: "I snuggled down under the covers, hugging my knees as tight as I could, and hoping he would stay at home all the time, instead of going off again. . . . It sure felt good being there in the dark with him" (205). The hug itself is a poignantly displaced gesture of need and affection. The book's final story, "My Old Man Hasn't Been the Same Since," concludes with two more gestures by William, this time openly expressed. When Martha informs Morris that he has just eaten College Boy, William is the first to speak out against her action: "'That was College Boy, Ma,' I said, 'you shouldn't—'" (238). Immediately after delivering this censure, he goes off into the night to seek his father, who has fled in horror from the fatal, fateful dinner: "I got up and went through the house behind him. . . . The cigar stub he had left on the porch railing when we went inside to supper was still burning, and it smelled just like my old man. I hurried down the steps and ran down the street trying to catch up with him before it was too late to find him in the dark" (238-39). In a reversal of roles from the earlier episode, William's presence will presumably now comfort Morris in the elder Stroup's hour of darkness. Together, the endings of these strategically placed and related stories reject the proposition that the narrator of *Georgia Boy* is too much the camera to convince as a human being. A camera neither feels nor grows.

Admittedly, there are no statements by William to match Huck Finn's ruefully enlightened pronouncement that "human beings *can* be awful cruel to one another" (290). Nor should there be any. The charm of *Georgia Boy* is that despite its candidly portrayed inhumanities, it is primarily an idyll of innocence. In a 1958 interview, Caldwell strongly suggested that he viewed *Georgia Boy* as a nostalgia piece: "I still have a feeling for a book I wrote. . . . It was a book called *Georgia Boy*, a series of sketches about a boy in Georgia growing up in company with his mother, his father, and a Negro playmate of the same age— growing up at that particular time in America when life was a little more leisurely and there was not so much compelling action put upon people" (Collins 44).

The author's own feeling, expressed here, for this allegedly mellow yester-year does much to explain the point of view in his book. While a grown man like Erskine Caldwell or even a sensitive teenager like Huck Finn might be expected to condemn social and economic wrongs, a younger boy may be permitted to describe them without rendering a verdict. To depict the Georgia of his fondly remembered boyhood as a kind of localized age of innocence, Caldwell required a narrator who was at an innocent age. The nostalgic ambiance of *Georgia Boy* mainly derives from the second word in its title, not the first. In 1980 Caldwell described as follows his erstwhile ambivalence toward the South: "As I was growing up, I did resent the South. I resented its economy and sociology. I resented the lack of opportunity in general, and especially the fact that the black people there were not accorded the same opportunity as the white people. . . . On the other hand, I would also say that, just like anyone who has a homeplace, I have always had a deep regard for this region. . . . I have always liked the South and liked its people, even though I had these qualifications because of some of the conditions there" (Broadwell and Hoag, "Writer First" 162). In other works Caldwell scourged his homeplace for its deprivations and its racism. In *Georgia Boy* he found a way, by using a narrator who had not yet had to grow up, to express his love without compromising his principles or distorting the historical record.

The facts in *Georgia Boy* speak for themselves, directly to the reader, without any needed proddings by William Stroup. Although there is no judgment pronounced about such reprehensible occurrences as the persecution of Handsome Brown, there is judgment amply implied. James Devlin cites "The Time Handsome Brown Ran Away" as a story calling for moral response with none forthcoming. In this episode, Handsome leaves the Stroups to join a carnival, where his dubious employment consists of offering his head as a target for baseball-throwing customers. Morris resents the absconding of his retainer and knocks Handsome silly with spitballs before leading him back to the fold. Clearly, this carnivalized brutality is no laughing matter. Neither does Caldwell present it that way: "The spit-ball hit him on the left side of the head with a sound like a board striking a bale of cotton. Handsome sank down to the ground with a low moan. 'Look here, mister,' the man in the silk shirt said, . . . 'I think you'd better quit chunking at this darkey. He'll be killed if this keeps up much longer'" (130). Although the story has its comic moments, the pointed description and dialogue here are sufficient proof that this scene is not meant to be one of them. Morris's *spit*balls are manifestly dangerous and demeaning.

Nor should we find funny the scornful racism of Uncle Ned Stroup, who takes exception to Handsome's request that he not be the one to tell Martha of her ne'er-do-well brother-in-law's arrival: "What you talking about, nigger! . . . Don't you never talk back like that as long as you live! One more peep out of you like that again, and I'll bash your head in with this rock! You hear me, nigger!" (215). Handsome's difficulties with goats and woodpeckers may be laughed off as pratfall vaudeville, defused by their exaggeration and improbability. Ned's threat of racist murder, however, is unmistakably malicious. Just as Caldwell's prose differentiates between outrageousness and outrage, so too must the reader. In the division of labor established by this book, other characters act and are acted upon, the narrator observes and reports with a naivete appropriate to his age, and the readers must decide when to laugh and when to shake their heads. *Georgia Boy* is a work involving children, not necessarily for them.

William Stroup is a Georgia boy, but the comprehensively apt title of this story cycle refers to more than him alone. There are three Georgia boys here, not one; and the separate responses required by each mark the range of reader responsibility to Caldwell's book. To be sure, William is still a little boy. In order to appreciate his view of Georgia we must understand the limitations of his youthful vantage point. Although the Georgia he depicts is Eden after, rather than before, the Fall, he himself is an Adam without meaningful knowledge of good and evil. As a result of his inchoate perception, the Georgia this boy gives us is at once idyllic without being ideal. Indeed, his own innocence is its principal saving grace.

Being both a youth and a black, Handsome Brown is doubly cast as a boy. When playing with his white friend William, Handsome, too, is an icon of childhood, that brief span before economics and sociology break up the games. But in the following stereotyped calumny by Uncle Ned, we are given another image of what it meant to be black and male, regardless of age, in early twentieth-century Georgia: "'I'll bet he ain't never done enough work, all told, to earn a day's board and keep,' Uncle Ned said. 'Ain't that right, boy?'" (214). Both the statement and the question address Handsome. When in the company of William Stroup and Handsome Brown, the reader is simultaneously present in two different Georgias and must respond appropriately to each.

So, too, does the extended boyhood of Morris Stroup call for a divided response. On the one hand, we like Morris just because he is such an unregenerate, though by no means unchastened, good old boy. We are drawn to him as to all the good-natured screwups who manage to prolong boyhood into middle age and in so doing do not lack for company. To this day in the South they are at once social pariahs and a prideful club, depending on the eye of the beholder. But while Morris behaves as if "boys will be boys" were his exemption from adult mores, Martha finally does not. All the years of his cockfighting, his philandering and his remorseless gallivanting have unraveled her to the point where she must either pull things together or let them come completely apart. The axe that claims the head of College Boy cuts off the boyhood of Morris as well, and to at least the half-hearted approval of the reader. A fitting end to the entire book, her decisive action also moves her son to the edge, if not the age, of judgment and the South, symbolically, to the brink of change.

In an important sense, there is still another boy present in *Georgia Boy*, never described or even mentioned but nonetheless haunting these Georgia scenes— haunting them, haunted by them. When Erskine Caldwell told an interviewer in 1986 that the stories here are "not in any way autobiographical" (Arnold 288), he almost certainly meant only that the specific incidents are fabrications and that his own stable parents had not stood as models for the elder Stroups. In 1983, however, Caldwell left no doubt that his personal experience of boyhood had been the inspiration for this book. After citing *Georgia Boy* as a favorite work, he described it as follows: "This was a whole series of short stories I wrote as the result of looking back at my early life and a playmate who happened to be a black boy. . . . That was a sort of landmark [for me] as far as writing was concerned, because I wrote it purely for the fact that I wanted to go back and think about my early life" (Kehl 239). Thus, even if *Georgia Boy* is not personal history, it is a kind of spiritual autobiography—the more significant of the two because that is the material of mythology, which we value above the historical record.

Not since before the revival of academic interest in Erskine Caldwell's writings over the last decade has *Georgia Boy* been available in a paperback edition. For classroom study, the book, in effect, does not exist. This essay has several functions. It is a petition to publishers to act *pro bono publico* by reissuing *Georgia Boy* in an accessible, competitively priced format. It is a recommendation to teachers to adopt this book for appropriate courses: "Southern Fiction"; "American Humor"; "The American *Bildungsroman*"; short-story, novel and historical surveys are among its logical contexts. Further, it is an invitation to students and all other readers to approach *Georgia Boy* with great expectations. Certainly, there are other works by Caldwell that deserve to be brought back. The novels *Journeyman* (1935), *Trouble in July* (1940) and *Tragic Ground* (1944) all have champions; and many voices have praised his early stories. The combinative advantages of the story-cycle form, however, set *Georgia Boy* apart from, and arguably above, these other works. It is distinguished, moreover, by a complex structural and stylistic weave and by the many variations on its major theme played by an instrumental narrator whose personal simplicity is the book's greatest sophistication. For these reasons and others, if I had to choose just a single Caldwell work for regeneration, I would unhesitatingly select the too long neglected *Georgia Boy*. In all likelihood, so would he.

NOTES

[1] Cowley cites as valuable "the novels up to *Trouble in July* (1940) and the stories up to *Georgia Boy* (1943)" ("Caldwell's Magic" 6-7). His assertion in "Two Caldwells" that *Trouble in July* is "the best [novel] that Caldwell has written"(199) demonstrates that his use of the ambiguous phrase "up to" is intended to be inclusive.

[2] The eight stories are "My Old Man's Baling Machine," "The Day We Rang the Bell for Preacher Hawshaw," "The Time Ma Spent the Day at Aunt Bessie's," "My Old Man and the Gypsy Queen," "The Time Handsome Brown Ran Away," "My Old Man and Pretty Sooky," "My Old Man's Political Appointment" and "Uncle Ned's Short Stay."

[3]Although he told one interviewer, in 1983, that in writing *Georgia Boy* he had in mind "no progressive thought, no beginning or end" (Bonetti 248), these words characterize his often-described and consistently-applied practice of organic creation. Thus, they do not distinguish this book from his other long fiction.

[4]Scott MacDonald mentions *Georgia Boy* in the introduction to his essay on repetition in Caldwell's stories; however, he does not discuss the book in detail (330).

[5]Twice in *Georgia Boy* we are told that Handsome Brown has been with the Stroups "since he was eleven years old" (128, 157). Caldwell, though, told Kehl that the two boys were modeled on himself and a friend who were "probably ten or twelve years old at the time" (239). In any case, William, especially, behaves as a still small boy rather than as an older youth.

WORKS CITED

Arnold, Edwin T., ed. *Conversations with Erskine Caldwell*. Jackson: UP of Mississippi, 1988.
_____. "Interview with Erskine Caldwell." Arnold, *Conversations* 265-96.
Bonetti, Kay. "A Good Listener Speaks." Arnold, *Conversations* 244-51.
Broadwell, Elizabeth Pell, and Ronald Wesley Hoag. "Erskine Caldwell on Southern Realism." Arnold, *Conversations* 200-04.
_____. "'A Writer First': An Interview with Erskine Caldwell." Arnold, *Conversations* 160-78.
Caldwell, Erskine. *Georgia Boy*. New York: Grosset and Dunlap, 1950.
_____. *Jackpot*. Cleveland: World, 1948.
Canby, Henry Seidel. "'Introduction' to The Pocket Book of Erskine Caldwell Stories." MacDonald, *Essays* 214-20.
Collins, Carvel. "Erskine Caldwell at Work." Arnold, *Conversations* 38-51.
Cowley, Malcolm. "Erskine Caldwell's Magic." *Pembroke Magazine* 11 (1979): 6-7.
_____. "Georgia Boy: A Retrospect of Erskine Caldwell." MacDonald, *Essays* 315-29.
_____. "The Two Erskine Caldwells." MacDonald, *Essays* 198-200.
Devlin, James E. *Erskine Caldwell*. Boston: Twayne, 1984.
Frohock, W. M. "Erskine Caldwell: Sentimental Gentleman From Georgia." MacDonald, *Essays* 201-13.
Guccione. "Sex, Sin and Society Through the Eyes of Erskine Caldwell." Arnold, *Conversations* 52-57.
Hooper, Johnson Jones. "Simon Plays the 'Snatch' Game." *Humor of the Old Southwest*. Ed. Hennig Cohen and William B. Dillingham. 2nd ed. Athens: U of Georgia P, 1975. 204-10.
Kehl, D. G. "Portrait of an American Primitive: A Conversation with Erskine Caldwell." Arnold, *Conversations* 233-43.
Korges, James. *Erskine Caldwell*. Minneapolis: U of Minnesota P, 1969.
MacDonald, Scott. "Repetition as Technique in the Stories of Erskine Caldwell." MacDonald, *Essays* 330-41.
_____, ed. *Critical Essays on Erskine Caldwell*. Boston: Hall, 1981.
Twain, Mark. *Adventures of Huckleberry Finn*. 1885. Berkeley: U of California P, 1985.

Interview with Helen Caldwell Cushman

HARVEY L. KLEVAR

Both of Erskine Caldwell's purportedly autobiographical works—Call It Experience *and* With All My Might—*scarcely hint at the existences of his first wife and
their children. Since the accounts represent attempts to chart his literary career,
Caldwell's failure to mention these three children—Erskine Preston, Dabney and
Janet—is perhaps understandable. But his failure to acknowledge either Helen or
her contributions to his early literary success is enigmatic.*

*Married to Caldwell from 1925 to 1938, Helen was much more than his wife
and the mother of his children. She was also his sole literary companion and critic
during what proved to be the most creatively productive period of his life. Her
recollections and reflections, therefore, are invaluable to those seeking an understanding of the man and his works.*

*No doubt, Helen Caldwell Cushman's interpretations and memories were as
personally selective and self-justifying as are all such reconstructions. Yet in every
instance wherein I was able to measure her accounting against other testimonies
and written evidence, I found it to be unusually accurate, astute and balanced.
Though she spoke candidly about both Erskine and herself four decades after the
fact, she accorded him a generous degree of grace and forgiveness.*

*During the course of my biographical research, I interviewed Helen on three
different occasions, twice at her residence in Mount Vernon, Maine, and once in
Beaufort, North Carolina, where she was visiting her daughter, Janet. The Mount
Vernon place—a large, rambling house built in 1778—was the only one she and
Erskine had called home during their thirteen years of marriage.*

*During my meetings with Helen—on 29-30 July 1977, 29 September 1978
and 23 January 1979—she was always congenially accepting, cooperative and
direct. In fact she seemed to enjoy the opportunity to share with others that life
which she and Erskine once had lived together. Seventy years old when I first
interviewed her, Helen was an extremely intelligent and vital person. Because I so
valued and enjoyed my meetings with her, I experienced a genuine sense of loss and
sadness when I belatedly learned of her death in the autumn of 1986. Some six
months later Erskine, like Helen, died a victim of cancer and emphysema.*

*Because our six hours of taped conversation was so loosely structured and
meandering, I have exercised some editorial license in selecting and formatting*

86

*portions to be included in the following transcription. In that process I have
excerpted those parts that seem most pertinent to understanding Caldwell as a
person and writer.*

HK: You first met Erskine at the University of Virginia.

HC: Yes. I must have been halfway along through my first year of graduate school,
in French, when I met Erskine.

HK: So you were still fairly young at this time?

HC: Oh yes. I wasn't eighteen yet. I married him when I was eighteen. I met
Erskine after a concert of Sergei Rachmaninoff. I always said I was seduced by
Rachmaninoff. I met Erskine and the first thing he said to me was—and I won't
use the word because I can't use four letter words very well—he said, "I'd like to
go to bed with you right now." Well, that was a little bit startling to me.

HK: You had never met him before and that's the way he introduced himself to
you!?

HC: That's what he said to me when he took me home after our first date, first
meeting. He said, "I'd like to knock you in the head with a rock and go to bed with
you."

HK: Was he the one who wanted to get married? Did he urge you to get married?

HC: Yes. I'll tell you why. He thought I might become pregnant because I was
sleeping with him by then.

HK: And so you eloped?

HC: Yes, to Washington, D.C. And the minute that I was married, I knew that I
had made a mistake. The first night of my marriage, my wedding night, Erskine
took me to five burlesque shows. Which was a little startling (*laughter*).

HK: Why do you think he did that?

HC: Oh, but this is the whole point, my dear. He had to prove himself. He had
been brought up by these old maid aunts and a very strict mother. Now, of course,
long hair is fashionable, but not in the days that he grew up, and he had long curls

Helen Caldwell, summer, 1934, Burbank, California.

Erskine Caldwell, summer, 1934, Burbank, California.

when he was eight years old. He had a great objection to "good women." That's why he wanted me to go to burlesque shows. I had to be led down the runway, you see, and do a striptease. I don't mind being an enthusiast at all, but it was all a bit shocking when you're eighteen. Now as I look back I can understand this in Erskine, and I feel sorry for him because in many ways he missed a great deal.

HK: Was he always a terribly private person?

HC: Yes, always. He never talked about himself as a child growing up, what he was feeling inside. I know he never liked Georgia. He hated Georgia. It was too oppressive. Part of it was not his fault. It was his mother's superior attitude toward the people in Georgia, these little back country towns. She was an FFV; she came from one of the finest families in Virginia and would never let you forget it. And no one was good enough to associate with her son. Erskine could never go to public school until he was eleven years old because Mrs. Caldwell didn't think that the people in these small towns where Father was the minister were fit to associate with him. So she brought Erskine up. He had these five old maid aunts, and this affected his sexual life, if you know what I mean. That's why he took me to the burlesque shows. (*Small laugh.*)

HK: In Wrens, Georgia, they still don't want to talk about Erskine. They want to talk about his mother and father.

HC: Everybody adored Erskine's father [Ira Sylvester Caldwell]. He was a magnificent, wonderful man. He was as near a saint as anybody I have ever known. He was kind. He would give anybody his shirt. He would do anything for people. But if ever I saw a man who was berated by a shrew, Father was by Mrs. Caldwell.

HK: When Erskine married you, he did not have an job. Is that correct?

HC: Yes, he was a student at the University. He was in my English class.

HK: How did you live?

HC: We lived on my parents. They had a house, and fed us and so forth.

HK: Then after that, his first job was with the *Atlanta Journal*?

HC: That's right. And he couldn't stand it. He wanted to write. That's true. Always be sure you have this: he had an overwhelming obsession to write. That was the one thing that mattered to him. The only thing that mattered, really. It mattered more than human beings by far. I always respected this in him. It was the one thing he really hoped to do in life. But he didn't write easily. Writing was very difficult for him. You know, some people can bat out something. But he could not. For him it was really an act of conceiving, the conception of a child for him. Everything that he wrote.

HK: He says today that he didn't revise. Is that true?

HC: No, he didn't often. I used to cut his work. I used to cut through with a big blue pencil. And I corrected his errors. When he was in the throes of creation, shall we call it, he was completely inapproachable, and nobody was allowed to make any noise in this house. And don't think that was easy, with two young children. I had to keep them out of the way. He wrote very painfully and was possessed to write. He had this internal compulsion. And I was truly interested in his work or I would have left him long, long before.

But I did think he had a great deal of talent; I still do. I think some of his books are excellent. Some I do not. I think his book about Maine, for example, *A Lamp for Nightfall*, is terrible. It had nothing to do about Maine. It's false. Unlike *Tobacco Road*, which is purely Georgia, or *God's Little Acre*, both of which I think are excellent. I edited most of his books during our marriage. That was one of the reasons I was most interested. I have always felt that he is a far better short-story writer than he is a novelist, and I credit myself to some extent since I don't think he's written a really good book since our divorce. It's the same picture over and over again.

HK: What else did you do besides edit? Did you ever give him ideas for stories? Would you tell him that this character doesn't ring true or that this scene isn't right?

HC: Not ideas necessarily. Most of his short stories written in those days were based on actual events in Mount Vernon, ''A Country Full of Swedes,'' and so forth. I did criticize his characters in what was originally *Autumn Hill*, later called *A Lamp for Nightfall*. It's an awful thing. I felt so sorry that it was ever published. And I'd have kept him from writing some of the trash that he actually wrote later, and I mean this sincerely, because I think he was capable of doing much more. But I don't think you could judge him by the same standards you'd judge an ordinary human being. You may quote me exactly. I think the very thing that made him a good writer was the very thing that removed him from the human equation. In other words, he was removed from ordinary behavior by his genius, if such it was. Look at Fitzgerald or Hemingway or Thomas Wolfe . . . any one of them. Or D. H. Lawrence, for that matter. Of course, he always had Frieda, who was a mother image to him.

Erskine and Helen Caldwell's home in Mt. Vernon, Maine.

HK: Did he ever talk about other authors? Did he ever say, "Now, that guy doesn't have nearly the talent I do"?

HC: No. I truly will say this. He was not malicious as far as people's writing was concerned. And, although he claims not to have read, the one writer I know he admired was Sherwood Anderson: he admired *Winesburg, Ohio* terribly. He also admired Theodore Dreiser and a few other writers and works you may not know. Edward Dahlberg's *From Flushing to Calvary*, for instance. And he admired Manuel Komroff. Erskine claims never to have read all these people, which is utterly ridiculous. I have all of D. H. Lawrence's first editions—one of the first books Erskine ever gave me was *St. Mawr*, and we read it together. We read all of D. H. Lawrence and he was terribly impressed by him, as he should have been, even his poetry, plus *Sea and Sardinia* and *The Plumed Serpent* which, of course, is not poetry. He read that although there is a lot about church in it, and I think that escaped Erskine. And one other writer he liked was Morley Callaghan, a very fine writer. But his main interest seemed to be in short-story writers. He wouldn't have appreciated reading Somerset Maugham, and I'm positive he couldn't read Aldous Huxley. He didn't have the vocabulary to read Huxley. But writers like Roark Bradford, Robert Cantwell, Ambrose Bierce, he liked. And a poet he respected, was devoted to, was Carl Sandburg, whom Erskine and I saw when we were in school and who was the most informal of all speakers.

HK: Before Erskine started being published, how did you get by financially?

HC: Oh, my family and his family. But it was very lean indeed. In the fall of 1929, Erskine's mother gave him some money for a trip to Hollywood. You know, he needed to travel and see the world. And when her brother died and she had a little money, Erskine borrowed it, I think. That's when we started the bookstore in Portland, which was not successful, incidentally.

HK: You had the children with you?

HC: I had them for a while, and then we sent them to Charlottesville, Virginia, where they stayed with my family. You see, I was working then in the bookshop and Erskine was writing. Then a girl who had graduated from Smith came up and Erskine fell in love with her, so I left and went to Virginia and after awhile I came back. I guess I brought one of the children back but not both. I can't remember. Later he lived with this girl. Sometime about 1931 he got sick of the bookstore, and it was about to go under anyway and we moved up here to Mount Vernon.

HK: The romance with the girl was over?

HC: Oh, yes. I mean, that was a passing fancy. There'd been others. Not romantic, but bed-partners, shall we say.

HK: Had his unfaithfulness at this time jeopardized your marriage?

HC: Well, you're going to accept it after a certain while. I mean, adultery pure and simple, you can cope with, I think. But if it involves deep feelings, and so forth, you can't. Anyhow, sometime in 1932 we went down to Georgia—it was too damned cold here—and went to see his father and mother. In the meantime, my father died. We had some money then, and Erskine stopped working entirely.

HK: How was it when Erskine was first published?

HC: This goes back a year or so before, when he first went to New York and I went with him to sign the contract with Scribner's. It may have been in late '31, possibly '32. We were staying at a crummy hotel run by a gangster. And so we walked over to Scribner's, which was on 5th Avenue, and he said, "Helen, you're too shabby. You'd better not come up." I should have told him something right then and there, but I didn't. I was meek and mild. I waited for him two and a half hours, and finally I took a taxi back to the hotel. He was so furious with me that he didn't speak to me for the rest of the time we were in New York City, for ten days, because I didn't wait until he deigned to come back out there.

HK: But you didn't make any money off *Tobacco Road* at first?

HC: No, we didn't. A year or so later, Erskine went to New York because *God's Little Acre* had been suppressed by John S. Sumner, who was head of the New York Society for the Suppression of Vice. And it was quite a trial. The book was found "not guilty." Well, anyhow, Erskine went on the bus, and he came back. Naturally, he was pleased. But meantime I was very upset because all of the money we had, which wasn't a great deal, was in the banks and Roosevelt had closed all the banks. It was the time of the Bank Holiday, and you couldn't get your money out of the bank for any good reason. I said to him, "What are we going to do? I don't know how we'll exist." He said, "Well, look at this." And he showed me a slip of paper. And it said on it, "Boston, to Akron, to St. Louis, to New Orleans." And I said, "What the hell does that mean?" He said, "I'm going tomorrow." I said, "What do you mean, 'I'm going tomorrow'?" He said, "Well, I have a job, and I'm going to replace William Faulkner for Metro Goldwyn. And I'm going to leave tomorrow." And so Erskine went on location in the bayous of Louisiana to do this screenwriting.

HK: Why was he replacing William Faulkner?

HC: Because Faulkner couldn't stand Hollywood. Faulkner said, "I can't write unless I go home," and he went back to Mississippi. So that's what Erskine was doing. Erskine went on. And so, from having maybe twenty dollars a week that my mother would send, or Mrs. Caldwell would send or something, all of a sudden Erskine was making $250.00 a week, which, I assure you, in 1933 was a fortune. But in those days we were hungry, and a writer always writes better when he's hungry. I believe this. And the minute he went to Hollywood, things started deteriorating, not as far as we were concerned but as far as his writing was concerned. I know he had friends like Dudley Nichols, who was a very good screenwriter, who used to warn him: "Don't let this happen to you. You'll get caught in the Hollywood affair and you'll go Hollywood, and you can never write again."

    When Erskine came back that fall *Tobacco Road* opened in New York, and we went down for the opening and from then on things were different. You know, I could go to Duff-Goodman and get a $700.00 dress without bothering.

HK: Were you both extravagant?

HC: No, no. Well, Erskine would always buy a car, but I was too afraid of him to do anything like that. The only thing I ever bought was books. And, of course, my mother and father always supported us. They owned the place. We didn't own the place. We never paid any rent, didn't even pay the taxes for awhile.

HK: Do you think Erskine loved you, Helen?

HC: Yes. In a way he did. He was dependent on me.

HK: But his infidelities, and then his abandoning you and the family for Margaret Bourke-White—?

HC: I don't know. Possibly it was a quest, a search. That's why he was so interested in having affairs.

HK: Nevertheless, the situation with Margaret Bourke-White still puzzles me. It certainly wasn't simply a sexual fascination, was it?

HC: Well, he certainly must have admired her work. But she was a very vital human being anyway. And she was the sort of person who, if she were to go on a trip with you—and you might have your wife and both children, that wouldn't matter—she would get into your bed before the night was out. That was the sort of thing she did. When Erskine first went with Margaret Bourke-White on this trip to do *You Have Seen Their Faces*, he hired his former secretary from Metro Goldwyn Mayer, Ruth Carnall, who had been his mistress, to go with them to keep the financial bit straight because Margaret Bourke-White was known to be unscrupulous financially, would take advantage of you, you see. I mean, that's what he thought. So, Ruth went along. And Ruth wrote me a blow-by-blow account of the affair before she left. She wrote me about Margaret's appearing without any clothes on in Erskine's room and losing her temper and pulling all of the fixtures out of the wall.

HK: How did you happen to know Ruth Carnall? Why was she writing you?

HC: She was a friend of mine. I knew her after she was his mistress. I didn't go to Hollywood during Erskine's first year; I was here. The second year I did go. So I knew her then and she'd go and visit with us and so forth. And, you know, when I first met Margaret, I liked her immediately. I had never seen her before and this was well along into their relationship. So Margaret said to me, "How would you like something to drink?" And I said, "Yes, I'll have some Scotch." And she said, "So will I." And she ordered a bottle. Erskine slammed his hand on the table. "I'LL BE GODDAMNED!" he said. "Now here I get Helen trained so she won't drink and I'm trying to train Margaret Bourke-White and you both defy me!" Well, we howled at that!

HK: Erskine told me that he never swore.

HC: Well, he did then. He would swear on occasion, but he wasn't terribly profane. Another time—this was the year that I was in New York and worked on his book [*You Have Seen Their Faces*]—I had to have an operation and my oldest son was going to Virginia to be with my mother. Erskine said, "I think you should send young Erskine home to Aunt Sally." That was his aunt. He said he did not want young Erskine to go home to my mother's because my mother allowed drinking in her place. And I said, "I will not." I said to him succinctly, "Between drinking and adultery, I think there's a little difference." And Reverend Caldwell was right there when I said it. I said, "Either young Erskine goes home to my mother or I'm not going to the hospital." I had an edema of the lung, which was very serious. I was unconscious for three days. I had a lung specialist in the middle of the night, and I had three nurses around the clock. And so finally I was just coming back into myself when Margaret Bourke-White came home from Alaska, and Erskine called up and told me everything that went on in their bed the night before.

HK: Why would he do this? Just to hurt you?

HC: Yes. That's his idea of paying me back for defying him. Also, he was afraid he was going to lose her. And this he had fear of several times, I know. Later, when they argued and she left him in Santa Fe, Erskine called for me to come out there and bring him back home. That was when Erskine wanted me to divorce him and name Margaret Bourke-White his correspondent. Then he thought she would have to marry him. But I said, "I will not wash your dirty linen in public." So that was that. But I did go so far, stupidly, as to drive him back from Santa Fe to New York. Jan was with me. She was a little girl then. And so I drove him back and then came home to Maine. But he was very upset emotionally and everything else then.

HK: Why did you stay with him as long as you did?

HC: Well. That's what I don't know.

HK: I can't understand how little money you got out of the divorce settlement.

HC: How stupid I was, you might say. Well, I had all I could take, and I wanted him to have no possible hold on me in any way whatever. As long as Erskine felt I was under his thumb, everything was all right. But after that time with Margaret Bourke-White and me, well, dammit, he lost control of both of us at once and that was outrageous.

HK: Was this a part of his southern background, where the man somehow thinks the woman should be subservient?

HC: I don't think so. I don't think he had many characteristics of the southern man. Of course, he always had this antipathy toward "good women" because he was hag-ridden by them for years.

HK: Did Erskine come back here to Mount Vernon to visit the children very much after the divorce?

HC: No, he was never here after the divorce. And, well, they didn't see that much of him in the year or two prior to the divorce.

HK: Did the children miss him very much?

HC: Not especially. He could be brutal to them.

HK: So Erskine was harsh with the children?

HC: Oh, yes. I feel sorry for Erskine now. He's missed a great deal—the succession of generations.

HK: The letters you wrote to Erskine pleading your and the children's needs were so moving, I just can't see how he could be so immune to what you were feeling. You *told* him; it was right there in black and white.

HC: Well, I know. But he was above reproach, dear friend. I mean by that, that this was his attitude. He really felt he was. And it would not have occurred to Erskine, for instance, that he was unkind to someone, because he didn't think that way. He could be abysmally rude, but I don't think he ever realized how much he was hurting somebody. Actually, I think he liked very few people. He would have been a better writer had he been more human, had he not removed himself so far from people that he could never understand them. This is the tragedy to me. He might have been truly great, but he lacked the personality to achieve his greatness.

Erskine and Virginia Caldwell, 1963. Photo courtesy of Dartmouth College Library.

Interview with Virginia Caldwell

EDWIN T. ARNOLD

I interviewed Virginia Caldwell at her home in Scottsdale, Arizona, in February 1988, approximately ten months after Erskine Caldwell's death.

ETA: What was your picture of Erskine Caldwell before you met Erskine Caldwell?

VC: Well, my picture of Erskine Caldwell before I met Erskine Caldwell (*laughter*) was that he was going to be a very conceited, ego-maniac type. I'd been invited to this dinner party, and everyone that I knew that had been invited was ecstatic, rushing about buying books—"Don't be late; Erskine Caldwell's coming"—and I thought, "Oh, what kind of a person will this be. He's getting all this adulation and attention." So I wore an old dress and I was late (*laughter*) because I've never thought great accomplishment makes a great human. It may make a great writer or great artist or great president, but there's a lot more that matters to me about a person—his character and his fundamentals. So I was not prepared to rush up and throw myself at his feet. I expected somebody who would dominate the conversation and let people come to him. And here was this wonderful, freckled, shy man who stayed in the background. We talked, and I thought, "Here *is* a wonderful person." I was tremendously impressed, and so was he.

ETA: Had you read any of his books before you met him?

VC: Well, of course I had read *Tobacco Road* and *God's Little Acre*, and had seen *Tobacco Road* on Broadway, but I wasn't forming my opinion of him from his writing. I was forming it from the way people acted and what I anticipated in a person who had that kind of attention. And he was shy and obviously a gentle person. Then I read some more, and in reading I found what I already had felt.

ETA: The years that you spent with Erskine were sometimes very trying years for him, in his career and his personal life. What was his attitude toward his writing and toward his career during those years?

VC: His attitude toward his writing and his career never changed in his lifetime. His writing was his life. He and his writing were inseparable in my mind. But, yes, there were some hard years after his divorce from June [Johnson, Caldwell's third wife]. He, of course, was paying alimony, and he had lost fifty percent plus of his property, and so he was starting over. He had a new wife to support. He was supporting one child completely and helping another one in college. I think it was inevitable that it would upset his work. When the divorce was going through, Erskine was so upset that he just packed up and went off. Nobody knew where he was. I didn't know where he was. He went to Mayo. For a fifty-three year old man to part with far more than half his security and still be weighed down with heavy monthly payments was a frightening thing, I'm sure. And how that affected his writing I think we can judge only by the kind of writing he did at that time. He was writing under duress. As somebody who didn't believe in divorce, getting a third one was not just an embarrassment but it went against his principles. Erskine was not a cheerful person by nature—humorous, yes, but there's a difference. He was dependent upon me for the good cheer, and he let me know early on that that was important to him, and so I turned into a Pollyanna, which wasn't much trouble— by habit or by instinct I'm that way anyway. And things got even worse when June began to sue him constantly. At first nothing came of these things. Finally one did go through, and we settled out of court just to get rid of the harassment because he wasn't able to do his best writing—he wrote, but he wasn't doing his best. So we had a long stretch there of what were difficult times, and it wasn't too long after we got that all worked out that he started to have health problems.

ETA: Was he aware that he was not doing his best work?

VC: You'd have to guess at this, because he never talked about it. He never said, "I just can't write" or "I'm having a terrible time with this because I'm so worried about what's happening with June and the lawyers." I think the only way you could know it was by the size of his wastepaper basket overflow and his disposition and his discouraged attitude. It showed up in his personality that he was not happy with some of the things that were going on in his life. But if he had been totally dissatisfied with what he was writing, I don't think he would have sent it to the publishers.

ETA: Well, how would he react to the generally harsh reviews his books received? Did he pay any attention to them?

VC: He really honestly did not pay much attention to the reviewers. I'm guessing that early on with all the criticism that he had, perhaps to survive it he had to turn it off. And I think he had turned it off in such a way that he didn't need it any more. You see, here I'm guessing; he never told me that. But a sensitive person; which Erskine was, maybe one of the most sensitive humans I've ever known, must have been terribly hurt. When he did his first writing he had deep feelings about it, the people and the sadness he was writing about, and then to have it laughed at or criticized or banned, what would that do to any sensitive man? It would hurt him so much that why go on paying attention to it? Just ignore it. That's my theory. During our thirty years of marriage he didn't pay any attention to the reviews. Now, when I would read good reviews, I would be excited and say, "Well, isn't this one in the *New Yorker* just great? I'd like you to see it." *In Search of Bisco* had the best reviews he had ever had. When he wrote *Close to Home* there were excellent reviews, and I can remember the idea that "the Old Caldwell is back and in good form again." Also for *The Weather Shelter* and *Summertime Island*. I was so happy when I read these reviews because, as a wife who is working as a team with her husband, it makes it extremely worthwhile to know that your husband is having success and that perhaps you're helping him a little to come back to the strong writing he is capable of.

ETA: Well, let me ask you how *you* reacted when you read these negative reviews. What were your feelings?

VC: I tended to reflect what I had picked up from Erskine. It didn't matter to him what the reviewers and the critics said. It was what the readers would say that was important to him, even though he did write for himself, as he always said. I do believe that he did, that he satisfied himself first. But then I think he liked to know that he gave pleasure to other people. This is something that I've thought about since Erskine died. Reviews continue to come in about *With All My Might* or various and sundry things being written about him, obituaries and articles connected with his death. And I can find that I get quite irate if something is negative, and I wouldn't have during his lifetime at all. I will write mental letters. I want to defend him. I suppose it's as simple as this: that perhaps he's not here to defend himself. So I reacted very calmly for thirty years, and now I don't.

ETA: What were your contributions to the writing of his books? Would you see them in typescript or would you see them only when they were published?

VC: He did his first draft on yellow paper, and he did a great deal of rewriting as he went, maybe one page a dozen times. But I would not see it until the first draft was finished, and then I did an edit on the first draft. Then he typed his perfect manuscript to send off.

ETA: Now when you say that you would do an edit, what would that consist of?

VC: Spelling, typos, perhaps a sentence that wasn't clear to me. It was a small edit.

ETA: You didn't make any suggestions concerning character or plot?

VC: It was a rare thing. My contributions were very minor, like putting salt in the soup.

ETA: Then he would incorporate your corrections?

VC: If he felt they were appropriate. And then he would type his A-One perfect manuscript with great care. And fascinating to me were the changes he made on the final draft. He would highlight things. I knew that was one reason that he didn't want anyone else to do his final draft. It was not just that he wanted to know how it was done and that it was perfect. It was also that he wanted to make changes that gave it a certain character.

ETA: How much do you think his reputation was hurt by the fact that he was not associated with one publishing company for a long period of time? He wasn't a house author with Scribner's, let's say, or Viking.

VC: I think the ultimate effect was devastating. I think that Erskine's reputation right now would be entirely different, would be much more secure in the academic field, if he had stayed with one publisher. I think it would have counted up to the time he was with Farrar, Straus. He was very happy there. It was a good relationship, and it was a boosting relationship. They had confidence and understanding. Some publishers just didn't understand him. And Farrar, Straus and their wonderful editor Bob Giroux understood Erskine, and when he was taken away from them, then he was left without a publisher.

ETA: What do you mean, "When he was taken away from them?"

VC: Well, Victor Weybright was, as you know, president of New American Library, and when they sold to the Times-Mirror, they didn't need Victor anymore, and he was kicked upstairs, to use the term. Victor was trying to hold his position, and he wanted to start a hardcover imprint for New American Library, and he wanted Erskine as one of his authors. We met him in Los Angeles, and he talked about their long and wonderful friendship and how it was because of Erskine that NAL had taken off. They had been the "good ol' team" and now they had a chance to start again in a whole new hardcover field. Erskine shouldn't have left Farrar, Straus, but actually Victor had a three-year contract with him for the rights to his books, which they then optioned for the hardcover. Erskine had already signed his contract, and he had no control over what Victor did. Victor was very persuasive and said that what he had decided to do was going to be good for Erskine. So Erskine didn't fight it, as he probably would have, because of the overtones of loyalty and friendship. Of course, the hardcover project went nowhere, and by that time Erskine had left Farrar, Straus, his last good stronghold.

ETA: How did he feel about the paperbacks with which he is so often associated, the cheap paperbacks with the lurid covers?

VC: He had no control over his covers, ever. And he didn't like them. But Erskine so often said that he was Presbyterian by nature, not by religion or belief, but by nature. And he didn't mourn, scratch and fight and complain as a lot of people do. If he didn't like a cover, that's what a publisher wanted and that's what they were doing and you accepted it. Erskine did not live with regret. He simply closed doors. It was just something that he had to live with.

ETA: How did Erskine come to write his autobiography, *With All My Might*?

VC: Pierre Belfont had lunch with us in Paris several years ago, and he said, "Erskine, why don't you write your autobiography?" and Erskine said, "Well, I already wrote one." And Pierre said, "But that's all about your work. Why don't you write one about yourself, your life other than your work?" And that was all that was said. And then we came back and Erskine wrote a letter to his agent then in New York and said, "Do you think it would be a worthwhile idea?" And she wrote back with great enthusiasm. That was what started it. I don't think he had it in his own mind to do it at all.

ETA: When he decided to do it, how deeply do you think he intended to examine his life?

VC: Well, you know how Erskine didn't like to talk very much. I think he just started writing and wanted to let the writing carry him. It's the only book that I ever worked on with him as he wrote it. By that I mean that I saw each chapter when he finished his writing and rewriting on that chapter, and I had never done that before on a book. With *Bisco* I had seen the first chapters and then I saw nothing after that, and that was *the* only other book I had ever looked at a page of until it was finished. I never even looked at the typewriter because I was superstitious. So

I saw three chapters of *Bisco*, and for *With All My Might* I read each chapter as he finished it. Erskine would start writing, and the next thing you knew he would be writing about his work. It was so terribly difficult for him to write about himself, his personal life. And so I would say, "Well, here we go again. Another *Call It Experience*. How about a little personal talk here?" And so he would go back and take out some of the work and put in more personality. That was my main contribution, to try to get it to the point where it did give you some idea of what he was like as a person.

ETA: Did he go back and look at letters, diaries, or was this all from his memory?

VC: It was all from his memory except for dates, and then we did get out the diaries we kept for the thirty years we were married. Before that he used his own memory.

ETA: *With All My Might* seems to break in halves. The first seems to be much more personal, and in the second half it seems to me you do get more business.

VC: That's true, and there are several reasons. One is that he was anxious to finish the book. He had the feeling that time wasn't going to last forever. The second was that he felt the book was already too long, so he was hurrying up the time span and the length, and he felt that he had to get the business parts in because, I think, he felt they were more important than the personality parts. I would have liked to see more of the personality parts because, just like any other reader, there were a lot of things that I never totally understood about Erskine. Still, for him, I think there is quite a lot of personal material in the book. I'm surprised that he put as much in it as he did. And, in the third place, writing it did take a toll on him. There were times after he had spent all day on it when he would come out of his study and just lie down on the floor in total exhaustion. That also happened with other books, but I think what *With All My Might* did to him was that at his age and in his general physical condition he needed to be moving around a little more. He had stopped riding his stationary bicycle; he couldn't take time to do that; he had to get this book done. And so he sat in that one position much too long, and he lost that small amount of activity that was so important, and I think that it hurt him physically.

ETA: How long did he work on it?

VC: He worked on it for a four-year period, or close to it. He had written a piece for Gale Research, who were doing an anthology of writers' autobiographies, and that was the nucleus, actually, that he pulled from when he moved on to the expanded work.

ETA: When did he name the book? Did he have his titles beforehand, or would he come up with them after he had written the books?

VC: He did it differently, but he was more apt to come up with them on the way. He would have a working title. With this one he came up with several titles and we talked about them, but neither one of us was satisfied with any of them. And then one day he went in and came back out with a sheet of paper, and on it he had typed WITH ALL MY MIGHT and said, "Well, what about that?" And it was so perfect.

ETA: You've suggested that he may have intuited that this could be his last book. Was there any physical reason during the writing of the book to suspect this? His last bout with cancer hadn't been diagnosed at this time, had it?

VC: No, it hadn't. But we had had an increasing number of signals that something might be going wrong. They tested the sedimentation rate, which shows infection or something else wrong in the blood, and every now and then his sed. rate would flare up and the Mayo doctors would put him through a whole string of tests. I remember one time they went all the way to the bone marrow because they were so certain that something was wrong. Also, very often he would suddenly run a high temperature, no reason for it; give him aspirin and it would come down. We had things like that going on all the time, and that might have been a signal to him. Remember what he said to you [in March, 1986], when he made that comment about living to be 83? And I said, "Oh, let it be 85. It's a better number," and he said, "Well, okay," to please me. But he had his 83 number in mind for some reason.

ETA: When did he finally discover that the cancer was back again?

VC: On July 22nd [1986], he said he was getting a cold. We were in Florida. He didn't tell me that he had a sore throat, because his lungs were really in just horrible condition. He had emphysema, he was getting fibrosis and he had only half of each lung to begin with. How he pushed himself to do what he did, I simply don't know. He had an incredible will power to keep going. Anybody else would have been out here sitting in the sun with those lungs. Anyway, we came home and it turned into pneumonia. Our doctor was out of town, and his substitute didn't have the knowledge to dig right into those Mayo contacts and compare x-rays. He put him in the hospital for six days and finally got the temperature down, but while all that was going on the cancer had started to incubate and boil over. They didn't find it on the first bronchoscopy, and we came home and he didn't get better, and then his regular doctor came home and sent him to another clinic here in Scottsdale, and they did another bronchoscopy and there it was. And they said, ''This time you've got a bad one. It goes like wildfire.'' And that was that.

ETA: He had been through lung cancer twice before. What was his reaction when they told him yet again, and that it was a bad one?

VC: His reaction was that we had to go to Paris, where *With All My Might* was being published in October. And this was September. (*Soft laughter.*) His first question was, ''If I take the chemotherapy, when will I be able to go to Paris?'' We were going on to Bulgaria after Paris to a writers' conference there. The doctors were going to let him go if he insisted, but they didn't like it. They told us they could lose control of the cancer and described all the things that could happen. He had to have oxygen on the plane and wheelchairs everywhere. He was on oxygen for eight months; he had a fifty-foot oxygen leash so he could go from one end of the house to the other, and he was never without it. So I called the publishers and they set up the oxygen, the airlines had all the oxygen arranged for, going and coming. And then he had an X-ray, and he had responded to the chemotherapy. And then they said, ''If you go, we will have to cut your chemotherapy, and the cancer may get out of control and that will be it. So it's up to you. Do you want to live longer, or do you want to have a fine trip?'' We were all going along with him, because it was his life and his book, and he is so completely loved in France that to be there for any occasion was very special. But he made the decision himself to try to extend his life. He gave up his trip to try to fight for his life. He went through chemotherapy for eight months. Alternate treatments were in the hospital. I went in, stayed with him; they put a cot in for me. And the other ones were in the doctor's office and then he came home. And he held up remarkably well until the seventh chemo. Then they gave him what they called a ''whammer,'' and then he lost his hair and became so weak that he could hardly get into the wheelchair.

ETA: When was this?

VC: He had the big one the end of February or the first part of March. And for a while we thought maybe it had worked; the x-rays showed improvements and some other symptoms were better, and we actually got happy, got out the champagne, thought we were beating it. But then they couldn't give him any more of the chemotherapy because his body couldn't tolerate any more of it after that time. And about three weeks passed and then all the old symptoms came back and then it was a fast one.

ETA: Did he talk about the fact that he was going to die?

VC: We always said, "If." We faced the fact that he might, and that his chances were not good. We faced that, and we were both aware of it. It wasn't a fantasy that everything was going to be all right. It was just trying to be totally strong and optimistic. One book that the doctor recommended we both read was on the practice of visualization, and Erskine said that he didn't need to see it. I insisted, and he said, "Well, I'll look at it." He read a couple of chapters and said, "It's just simple Christian Science," and he didn't read any more. But we certainly did try to do all the mental agility programs that we could think of, and perhaps it helped. Eight months was a long time to survive with that particular cancer at his age. The Mayo doctors were in touch all the time too because he was their prize patient. He had broken all kinds of records. I think a lot of other people would have sat back and more or less given up and not pushed the way he did. He was up at his desk on Tuesday and he died on Saturday [11 April 1987]. He was so weak that my son had to lift him into the wheelchair. On Wednesday morning he was up and dressed—I dressed him; he couldn't shave or do anything like that; he had lost all strength—and Drew lifted him into the wheelchair. I gave him his breakfast and he sat there a few minutes and then he said, "I'm going to have to go back to bed." And that was that. But up until then he wouldn't have breakfast in bed. He said, "If you stay in bed one day, then it's going to be the next day, and then you won't get up again."

ETA: He was working during those months? Writing?

VC: Writing letters, paying bills. When his hand reached the point it was so shaky it was illegible, he would take the check stubs out and put them in the typewriter and type them in.

ETA: And giving interviews. When did the *Washington Post* reporter, Charles Trueheart, come to visit?

VC: I think it was February, it might have been March, because it was connected with the book, of course. And then *USA Today* sent a reporter who came the week after Charles Trueheart did, and then they sent a photographer. The photographer came, and Erskine sat at the desk. He had lost his hair by that time, and he had a cap on his head. And when the man left, Erskine said, "I'm exhausted. All I did was sit here, and I'm exhausted." He said it in a kind of amazement. He wasn't complaining. It was just, "How can this be true, that I could be tired from just sitting here?"

ETA: After he went to bed on Wednesday, he didn't get up anymore.

VC: Yes. Erskine had said about a month before that Drew—Drew is my son—should come down and take care of some matters he wanted looked after. So Drew came in on Sunday afternoon, and Erskine had been taking his rest. He said to Drew, "Get a notebook and a pencil; I have a list." And the first thing on the list was to call several mortuaries and find the least expensive, which was just like him. But we did *not* take the least expensive. And this gave me an opening to talk to Erskine, who had always said that he wanted to be cremated and wanted his ashes scattered on the water: he didn't care what water, just any body of water. I had told him that I couldn't do it, that it went against something in me. But now I said to him, "Erskine, if something happens, do you still want to be scattered on the water?" And he said, "No, that's a silly idea. Probably the best thing to do would be to find a shovel, find a dead-end street, and dig a hole." And I said, "A dead-end street?" And he said, "Well, isn't that appropriate?" with a smile.

ETA: And so that sense of humor was still there.

VC: It was still there the night before he died. Our next-door neighbor is a psychiatrist, a dear and wonderful person. He and his wife did an awful lot of caretaking for us during that long year. And I felt that Erskine was slipping fast: he could hardly speak and his feet and fingers were turning blue. So I called our neighbor, and I said, "I'm frightened. I think Erskine is much worse tonight." So he came in and went and stood by the bed and said some proper thing, and Erskine looked up at him and you could hardly understand what he was saying, but what it was—was, "What are you charging for house calls?" So that was his humor, and by Saturday he wasn't talking. He nodded his head yes or no, but he couldn't talk. He was completely conscious, and he would not take pain pills or sleeping pills. He would just shake his head no.

ETA: Why do you think he wouldn't take these pills?

VC: Well, I'm very curious about it, because by then he did have pain. It had metastasized by then and he was in pain. It is very interesting to me that he wanted to be aware of everything. . . . That's probably the answer, that you want every moment of life. There was a great stoic strength about Erskine, a tenacity and determination. During all his surgery, whatever went wrong with him physically, he never complained. So of course he would go into death with fortitude. He died here in this house. He had his whole illness, except for those few nights in the hospital, at home and that's the way he wanted it.

ETA: What do you think of Erskine's reputation today? How much did his success finally cost him?

VC: Well, I think that the academics in his peer group never lost their respect for his work. I think as time went on and new and younger people came in, and writing changed so completely, that he lost an academic foothold at that time. I believe that he was in the process of retrieving it during those last few years before his death, when he was given the various medals, the French honor and the others that he received when he was elected to the Academy of American Arts and Letters. I believe that things were rolling back again. So I don't think that his popularity actually in cost could be estimated because I think if he'd lived a little longer he probably would have finished it out even higher than he will. We might protect his estate now. Having thought so much about this in the last year I would like to think that this whole pattern will continue and that he will make a whole turnabout.

Erskine knew what he was doing with his writing. I don't think that he slipped into something. I think he forced his writing, or *forged* it would be a better word. And I think he knew what he was doing for a great part of the years of his writing. Perhaps right at the beginning he didn't anticipate the impact or the reaction, but certainly after the first time he knew, and he went on doing it his way. And I think I have to believe what he told me. The day after our wedding we were leaving the Riverside Hotel in Reno, and the doorman saw his nametag on the suitcase and said, "Mr. Caldwell, may I shake your hand? Your books have given me so much pleasure." And so he shook hands and climbed into the taxi and said to me, "I'd rather have one comment like that than all the critics." Well, he must have meant that. So if he did not feel let down at the trend that his work took, then did it cost him anything? Perhaps we could speculate and say, "Well, perhaps he could have had the Nobel Prize." Well, I long ago lost count of the people who said to me that he should have had it for his first five books—Saul Bellow was one. If he felt satisfied, then I don't think we have a cost problem, do we?

ETA: Why do you think his reputation has remained so high in Italy and France, Russia and Japan, but has fluctuated so much in the United States?

VC: Actually, there is something here to which I would like to give a balance. I don't think that Erskine's reputation in Russia is that high. I think that for a while he was one of the popular authors, but *God's Little Acre* has never even been published in Russia. I don't think that he begins to be as popular as some of our other top American writers. And yet that is said about him so often. I question that. He had the same reception that John Steinbeck had and Hemingway would have had, if he had gone. Certainly we have been there with Hemingway posters plastered all over the place, and other writers who are very popular there. So Erskine was just one of the group; he wasn't anything outstanding. Now in Poland, it's a different story: he is extremely popular in Poland, but I don't think it has anything to do with the Communist ruling in Poland. It's just the people. People in Spain, for instance, told us that parts of Spain were almost like *Tobacco Road*: "We understand your husband's work because we have lived like that." People in Yugoslavia also say that. Bulgaria is another place where we were invited into the homes of professional people, and they lived in one room with a bathroom and did their cooking in the bathroom. They would tell me, "We feel free to invite you and your husband because we know he understands poverty. We'd be embarrassed to invite somebody from the Embassy because they've never seen people live like this." So possibly some of the liking could be from that. But I don't think that accounts for all of the popularity.

And I know this. He never deliberately wrote a book to fulfill a contract. Number one, his contracts had no deadline. He'd have a three-book contract, but he could have taken thirty years to fulfill it, so he had no pressure on him there. It's just that Erskine had to write. When he would say that he didn't know how to do anything else, he meant it. He was not an idle or lazy person. His travels had meaning to him only in that they connected with his work. The car trips that he loved to take were "book hunting" trips. He was just drifting, floating, hoping that something would come flying through the air that would give him the germ of an idea. He had to write. He could travel for just so long, and then he had to get back to that writing. It was a necessity for him.

Notes on Contributors

EDWIN T. ARNOLD is a professor of English at Appalachian State University. He is the co-author (with Eugene Miller) of *The Films and Career of Robert Aldrich* and editor of *Conversations with Erskine Caldwell*, which includes his own 1986 interview with Caldwell.

SYLVIA J. COOK teaches in the English Department at the University of Missouri-St. Louis. She is the author of *From Tobacco Road to Route 66: The Southern Poor White in Fiction*, and of articles on southern, proletarian and feminist fiction in the 1930s. She has just completed a study of Erskine Caldwell and is currently working on a book about poverty in American fiction.

JOHN HERSEY is the Pulitzer Prize-winning author of such American classics as *A Bell for Adano*, *Hiroshima*, *The Wall* and *White Lotus*.

RONALD WESLEY HOAG is an associate professor in the English Department at East Carolina University. He is co-author of a three-part interview with Erskine Caldwell that appeared in *Paris Review*, *Georgia Review* and *Mississippi Quarterly*. He also wrote the Caldwell chapter for *Fifty Southern Writers After 1900* (Greenwood Press). His other publications include articles on Henry Thoreau, Mark Twain, William Faulkner and John Updike.

WILLIAM L. HOWARD teaches English at Chicago State University. His dissertation was on Erskine Caldwell's early novels, and he is presently working on a critical study of Caldwell's fiction.

FUJISATO KITAJIMA is a lecturer at Kyoritsu Women's Junior College in Japan. He has translated *Trouble in July* and a number of Caldwell's short stories. He has also published *Erskine Caldwell, A Bibliography in Japan (1932-1981)* and *Erskine Caldwell, A Chronology (1903-1985)*.

HARVEY L. KLEVAR is a professor of anthropology at Luther College. He has researched Caldwell's life for over ten years and is finishing work on a biography entitled *Solitary Puritan*.

HENRY TERRIE is Professor Emeritus and former head of the English Department at Dartmouth College. He has published a previous article on "Erskine Caldwell's *Journeyman*: Comedy as Redemption" in the Erskine Caldwell issue of *Pembroke Magazine* (1979).

Index

American Academy of Arts and Letters, 109
Anderson, Sherwood (*Winesburg, Ohio*), 10, 73, 75-76, 80, 92
Andrews, Dana, 65
Aomi, Miyoko, 44
Atlanta Constitution, 10
Atlanta Journal, 10, 19
Augusta Chronicle, 10

Barton, James, 66
Belfont, Pierre, 103
Bellow, Saul, 109
Bierce, Ambrose, 43, 45, 92
Bode, Carl, 50
Bond, Ward, 63
Bourke-White, Margaret (second wife), 11, 12, 22-28, 42, 49, 50, 95-97
Bradford, Roark, 92
Burke, Kenneth, 12-13
Byrd, William, 80

Caldwell, Caroline Bell (mother), 9, 16-18, 23, 89, 90, 93
Caldwell, Dabney (second son), 86
Caldwell, Erskine, works: *Afternoons in Mid-America* (travel book), 34; *All Night Long* (novel), 27, 28, 40; *All-Out on the Road to Smolensk* (nonfiction), 26-27; *American Earth* (stories), 21, 43, 51; *Annette* (novel), 15, 33, 57; *Autumn Hill* (unpublished novel), 91; *The Bastard* (novel), 11, 20, 44, 52; "Blue Boy" (short story), 54; *Call It Experience* (autobiography), 44, 53, 86, 104; "Candy Man Beechum" (short story), 12; *Certain Women* (stories), 56; *Claudelle Inglish* (novel), 43, 56, 57; *Close to Home* (novel), 101; "Country Full of Swedes" (short story), 12, 91; "Crown Fire" (short story), 44; *Deep South* (nonfiction), 34; *The Deer at Our House* (children's book),

34; "The Empty Room" (short story), 43; *Episode in Palmetto* (novel), 51, 56; *Georgia Boy* (stories), 15, 27-28, 40, 45, 47, 50, 52, 56, 73-85; *God's Little Acre* (novel), 11, 12, 15, 21, 30, 36, 40, 43, 47, 49, 53-54, 60, 67-70 *passim*, 73, 91, 94, 99, 109; *God's Little Acre* (film), 67-70 *passim*; *Gretta* (novel), 15, 43, 44, 51, 56, 57; "The Growing Season" (short story), 54; *Gulf Coast Stories* (stories), 43, 56; *A House in the Uplands* (novel), 43, 44, 49, 51, 56; *In Search of Bisco* (nonfiction), 9, 34, 44, 101, 103-04; *Jackpot* (stories), 26, 51, 76; *Journeyman* (novel), 21, 22, 43, 49, 54, 84; *Kneel to the Rising Sun* (stories), 21, 45, 51; "Kneel to the Rising Sun" (short story), 12, 43; *A Lamp for Nightfall* (novel), 11, 91; *The Last Night of Summer* (novel), 57; "The Lonely Day" (short story), 44; *Love and Money* (novel), 15, 32-33, 43; "Midsummer Passion" (short story), 11; *Mission to Moscow* (film), 27; *Molly Cottontail* (children's book), 34, 44; *Moscow Under Fire* (nonfiction), 26; *North of the Danube* (nonfiction), 24; *Poor Fool* (novel), 44, 52; *Russia at War* (nonfiction), 26; *The Sacrilege of Alan Kent*, 18, 31, 32, 33, 52, 76; "Saturday Afternoon" (short story), 54; *Say, Is This the U.S.A.* (nonfiction), 26; *Some American People* (nonfiction), 44; *Southways* (stories), 36, 51; "The Strawberry Season" (short story), 44; *Summertime Island* (novel), 51, 101; *The Sure Hand of God* (novel), 15, 43, 49; *This Very Earth* (novel), 43, 44, 56; *Tobacco Road* (film), 62-68 *passim*; Tobacco Road (novel), 11, 12, 15, 21, 28, 36, 40, 42, 43, 49, 52, 54, 56, 59, 60-67 *passim*, 73, 77, 79, 91, 94, 99, 110; *Tobacco Road* (stage), 21, 59, 60-62, 94,

99; *Tragic Ground* (novel), 28, 43, 51,
54-55, 56, 84; *Trouble in July* (novel),
24-26, 43, 49, 53, 54, 84; "Vick Shore and
the Good of the Game" (short story), 44;
We Are the Living (stories), 21, 43, 51; *The
Weather Shelter* (novel), 38-39; 101; *With
All My Might* (autobiography), 12, 86, 101,
103-05, 106; *Writing in America*
(nonfiction), 51, 52; *You Have Seen Their
Faces* (nonfiction), 23, 24, 95, 96
Caldwell, Erskine Preston (first son), 19, 86
Caldwell, Ira Sylvester (father), 9, 16, 18, 19,
24, 90, 96
Caldwell, Janet (daughter), 23, 86, 96
Caldwell, June Johnson (third wife), 11,
27-31, 33, 100
Caldwell, Virginia Fletcher (fourth wife),
11-12, 31-34, 37, 40, 99-110
Callaghan, Morley, 92
Canby, Henry Seidel, 47, 75
Cantwell, Robert, 92
Capp, Al, 80
Carnall, Ruth, 95
Charlotte Observer, 10
Chaucer, Geoffrey (*Canterbury Tales*), 76
Clemens, S. L. (Mark Twain), 21, 47, 75, 80;
Adventures of Huckleberry Finn, 81
Collins, Carvel, 68
Contact, 49
Cowley, Malcolm, 15, 50, 51, 74-75
Crane, Stephen, "The Bride Comes to Yellow
Sky," 80
Cushman, Helen Lannigan Caldwell (first
wife), 10, 11, 18-24, 27, 28, 70, 86-97

Dahlberg, Edward, *From Flushing to Calvary,*
92
Daniels, Jonathan, 49
Dartmouth College, 36-41
Devlin, James, 56, 75, 79, 82
Dos Passos, John, 13, 42
Dreiser, Theodore, 26, 92; *Sister Carrie,* 10
Duell, Sloan and Pearce, 26, 27, 36

Ellison, Ralph, 59
Erskine Caldwell Literary Society, 46
Erskine College, 10, 18

Erskine, Ebenezer, 10

Farrar, Straus, 102, 103
Farrell, James, 42
Faulkner, William, 13, 15, 42, 43, 44, 45, 94
Fawcett, Roscoe, 30
Fitzgerald, F. Scott, 44, 91
Fletcher, Drew (step-son), 107, 108
Ford, John, 62, 66
Freeman, Mary Wilkins, "The Revolt of
Mother," 80
Frohock, W. M., 75

Gale Research, 104
Gannet, Lewis, 15
Gilroy, John, 39
Giroux, Bob, 102
Gordon, Caroline, 30
Gramatky, Hardie, 40
Grapewin, Charlie, 63

Hackett, Buddy, 68
Harris, George Washington, 21
Hawthorne, Nathaniel, 53
Hemingway, Ernest, 13, 15, 26, 42, 43, 44,
46, 91, 109; *In Our Time,* 10
Hench, Atcheson, 20, 41
Heron Press, 20
Hollywood, California, 94
Holman, C. Hugh, 49, 57
Hooper, Johnson Jones, 80
Hound and Horn, 49
Hull, Henry, 63
Huxley, Aldous, 92

Imai, Hajime, 44
Imanaga, Kaname, 44
Ito, Sei, 43

James, Henry, 43
Jefferson Reporter, 10
Johnson, Nunnally, 62, 66

Kaiko, Ken, 47
Kansas Writer's Conference (1948), 31
Kato, Osamu, 44